# Weird, Wacky and Wild

# MINNESOTA TRIVIA

Jeff Neidt & Lisa Wojna

Illustrations by Roger Garcia, Peter Tyler,
Patrick Hénaff, Roly Wood & Graham Johnson

BLUE
BIKE
BOOKS

D0288333

The Publisher: Blue Bike Books

Website: www.bluebikebooks.com

**Library and Archives Canada Cataloguing in Publication**

Neidt, Jeff, 1982–

Minnesota trivia : weird, wacky and wild / Jeff Neidt and Lisa Wojna.

ISBN-13: 978-1-897278-33-8

ISBN-10: 1-897278-33-0

    1. Minnesota—Miscellanea.  I. Wojna, Lisa, 1962–  II. Title.

F606.6.N43 2008               977.6               C2007-906366-7

*Project Director:* Nicholle Carrière
*Project Editor:* Kathy van Denderen
*Production:* Alexander Luthor
*Cover Image:* Courtesy of Sherwoodimagery/Dreamstime.com; photographer, Ronald Sherwood. Split Rock Lighthouse on Lake Superior, north of Duluth, MN.
*Illustrations:* Roger Garcia, Peter Tyler, Patrick Hénaff, Roly Wood, Graham Johnson

We acknowledge the support of the Alberta Foundation for the Arts for our publishing program.

PC: 01

# DEDICATION

This book is for Janet and my parents; you always knew what to say to keep me going, and for that I cannot thank you enough.

*–JRN*

# ACKNOWLEDGMENTS

First, I must thank my parents. Without you, this book quite literally would never have been written. For the obvious reason, yes—but also because your advice and patience over the years made me the man I am today. Don't worry about me; no matter where I go, in my head there is a worker, toiling at his craft; in my chest there is the soul of a Minnesotan, not taking a moment for granted.

Second, thank you to Janet. Without you, this book and my life would be hopelessly floating toward oblivion. Your passion for all that you do drives me each day to be a better person. You are a far better editor, researcher, friend and lover than I deserve. Each time I see you, I am reminded how blessed I am.

Thanks to Grandpa McManamon; I only wish for one more day with you so you could read this book. I hope it makes you proud. I send my regards to Grandpa Neidt for passing on his literary talents. To the rest of my family and friends—thank you for putting up with my incessant requests for stories, facts and anecdotes. Your names may not be mentioned, but there is a little bit of you on each page.

Of course, I must thank the teachers who inspired me over the years. Tom Hagel (who knows more about Minnesota than I could ever hope to know, even if I were to write 10 books); Robert Hackney and Barb Lambert for teaching me to write; Eliot Wilson for mentoring me as a writer and for not taking no for an answer—you are all inspirations beyond anything I have told you before. A hearty thanks goes to the teachers I work with, especially Paul Wieland, Mara Corey and Becky Haven— thank you for your mentorship in teaching and life. And of course, thank you to the students; you were there for laughs on the longest days.

Also, thank you to my publisher for taking a shot on a kid from Minnesota with loads of passion, but few bylines. And to my editor, Kathy van Denderen, who took my semi-coherent musings and made them the book you see before you.

Finally, thank you to the following people or things: Sam Adams for providing the beer I drank while writing the book; Nick Hornby and Dave Eggers for writing the two books that inspired me to write—if it weren't for your work I would probably be an accountant, and no one wants that; Polydream for your friendship, creative inspiration and for providing the music this book was written to; and to anyone else who asked me how "the book" was coming and reminded me to get working. I hope you enjoy.

*—JRN*

Many thanks to our clever editor, Kathy, who pieced together the work of two authors and did so seamlessly; to my co-author, Jeff, and to my family—my husband Garry, sons Peter, Matthew and Nathan, daughter Melissa and granddaughter Jada. Without you, all this and anything else I do in my life would be meaningless.

*—Lisa*

# CONTENTS

# INTRODUCTION

*It's a swell state, Minnesota.*

–Judy Garland

Growing up in Minnesota, I always thought it was a great state. Of course I did; it was the only state I knew. Well, there was Wisconsin, but my parents loved me and didn't let me cross the border. When it came time for choosing colleges, I harbored dreams of being my own Nick Carraway and moving off to the good life on the east coast. But I soon realized the jazz age was dead, and I am allergic to Ivy. I settled on the place that sums up all of Minnesota: St. Olaf College.

While at St. Olaf, I took a study abroad trip to Paderborn, Germany. That trip was formative to me writing this book in three ways. First, quite understandably, it made me appreciate home—specifically, the friendly, easygoing nature of Minnesotans. Every day in Minnesota feels as though you are in an episode of a 1950s sitcom, one where everyone says things such as "Swell!" and "That's great!" (for added effect, place extra emphasis on the "great," and smile as if you have Vaseline on your teeth). The weather may be cold, but you won't find a warmer group of people anywhere in the world than those in Minnesota.

Second, it made me realize just how Minnesotan I am. I am a mutt: Irish, German, French and Swedish. But my mixed heritage is what typifies me as a Minnesotan (OK, if I were a bit more Scandinavian it would help me to fit in better, but I do what I can). This is a state that took the best of its ancestors and made a hybrid. We took the Irish and German work ethic, Swedish patience, and well, still not sure what we used from the French. In addition, my years in Minnesota made me rely on my local comforts—I needed Target; I needed my Twins and Wild.

Finally, on a trip to Mallorca, Spain, I met a British girl. After a few drinks, we started talking about where we were from. I couldn't tell you where she is from (I think it ended in either -ford or -ham), or what she looked like from the shoulders up, but I do remember one peculiar question. She asked me, in what I can only guess was honesty, if all Minnesotans lived in igloos. Clearly, she had to be joking. My response of, "Yes, but it is hard in the summer when they melt and we are all homeless," did nothing to arouse her suspicions; she just went on nodding and gave me the sad eyes, usually reserved for commercials with starving children. Although not all people are as ignorant as my British friend, the more I traveled, the less I found people knew about Minnesota. Even in the United States! I am sure Manitoba is a nice place, and moose make great pets, but when your out-of-state friends think you live there, it makes you a bit angry!

So I resolved to be Minnesota's trumpeter. I would toot Minnesota's horn, or in a more fitting image of Minnesota, sound the bell in a church's handbell choir (yes, those do exist; check one out sometime—usually that many people in white robes means someone is about to die). I would be Minnesota's Scarlet Letter. I would tear down stereotypes as if they were the Berlin Wall. This book represents my humble effort to do that. I don't claim to know everything about the state or its culture—I'm not even Lutheran!—but I am willing to share what I do know.

And, if nothing else, after reading this book, please know that not all Minnesotans live in igloos. Some of us live in Ice Palaces.

*–JRN*

# MAGNIFICENT MINNESOTA

Welcome to Minnesota, pleased you could make it. First things first. There aren't 10,000 lakes; there are actually over 15,000. Yes, I know what the license plates state—what can I say, Minnesotans are humble to a fault. Let's just agree that there's a lot of water, beautiful "sky blue water." That water is the life-blood of the state. In the beginning, it powered Minnesota's industry; today it powers the state's adventuresome spirit. Only a state as powerful as Minnesota could give birth to the mighty Mississippi.

Minnesota isn't often mentioned when you think of great places to live. Why not? What do you want in a state? Vibrant night-life? Check out downtown, uptown or Dinkytown Minneapolis on a Friday or Saturday evening. A weekend getaway? Try a bed-and-breakfast on the bluffs of the mighty Mississippi in Red Wing. A week alone living out your transcendentalist dreams? The Boundary Waters Canoe Area is about as remote an area as you can get in the United States. Strong education? Try to find a state that features a better education system than Minnesota. Health care? Minnesotans are among the healthiest people in the country. And if you do get sick, there is the Mayo Clinic. If the clinic can treat world leaders, I'm sure it can treat whatever ails you. Did I mention the shopping, sports teams and numerous roadside attractions? You will probably want to check those out, too.

And what about the people? Well, that's the best part. Minnesotans are inventive people—folks who take the phrase "when life hands you lemons…" to a whole new level of meaning. Except that Minnesotans were handed really cold weather, and instead of making lemonade, they made snowmobiles and ice skates. Minnesotans are also polite, simple and unassuming people, which might explain why you may not know a lot of the things in this book. Minnesota is the best kept secret in the United States, and Minnesotans wouldn't have it any other way. In fact, most Minnesotans would be unhappy with this book—they don't want "out of towners" coming to destroy their paradise. But you know what? Come anyway. Minnesotans are so nice they will welcome you into their homes, invite you to church and make you hot dish. It's the Minnesota way.

*When I was younger, I remember hearing people say that "those who are born in Minnesota, stay in Minnesota." While I believe this is not true for all, I believe that Minnesota is a place that always calls you home. It is easy to find comfort in all that surrounds us here. And, after all, who can compete with 10,000 lakes?*

–Jessica, Park Rapids

# HAIL, MINNESOTA

*Minnesota, hail to thee!*
*Hail to thee our state so dear!*
*Thy light shall ever be*
*A beacon bright and clear...*

Who knew that when Truman Elwell Rickard first composed the music for these words for a University of Minnesota play in 1904 that they would become the basis for Minnesota's official state song? By all accounts the song was a hit, as far as the play went. But the following year, university president Cyrus Northrop asked another student, Arthur E. Upson, to make a few changes. In particular, Northrop wanted the line "Hail to thee, our Prexy Sire!" changed and a second verse added. The end result is the song we have today, but it wasn't bestowed with the status of official state song until April 19, 1945.

Truman Elwell Rickard, who initially wrote the words and music to "Hail, Minnesota," lived to see the day his creation was named the official state song. Arthur E. Upson, who reworked part of the piece and added another verse, did not. He died in 1908.

## All in the Name

"Minnesota" is a variation of the Dakota Native American word *mnishota*. Literally translated, *mni* means "water," and *shota* describes the hue. *Mnishota* therefore translates to "sky-tinted water" or the wonderfully obtuse "somewhat clouded water." The local Dakota Natives gave the name to the river; a phonetically challenged politician changed the spelling and applied it to the whole state.

DID YOU KNOW?

Minnesotans honor the Dakota people by naming a lot of random things after their word for water. There is Minnehaha Falls (which has nothing to do with laughing water, no matter what you may hear), Minneapolis and Minnetonka.

**Also Known As**

As with any other state, Minnesota sports several unique monikers:

- The North Star State—this name likely evolved from the state's motto, "L'Etoile du Nord," or "Star of the North."

- Land of 10,000 Lakes—referring, of course, to the many lakes in Minnesota. The claim is proudly displayed on the state license plates. However, any card-carrying Minnesotan would be happy to tell you that there are actually 15,291 lakes, each measuring larger than 10 acres.

- The Bread and Butter State—this nickname boasts what folks in this neck of the woods believe to be the state's superior grain and dairy industries. The term was first coined in New York in 1902, during the Pan-American Exposition.

- The Wheat State—again, this name points to Minnesota's lush wheat crops—and Minnesotan's creativity in coming up with nicknames.

- The Gopher State—after the striped creatures abundant in Minnesota.

## The Great Seal

Minnesota's Great Seal bears the image of a farmer plowing the earth, a Native American on horseback and an image of the Mississippi River, bannered by the state motto "L'Etoile du Nord." The seal is dated 1858, which was when Minnesota

gained statehood, but didn't become official until 1961. As with any other state seal, Minnesota's has undergone changes through the years, but the current version was legislated in 1983.

## DID YOU  KNOW?

The first version of the Great Seal depicted a Native American galloping east, not west, into the setting sun. The Latin phrase *Quo sursum velo videre* ("I want to see what lies beyond") represented the pioneer heritage of Minnesota, but unfortunately the Latin phrase was misspelled.

## State Flag

The scenes represented in the state seal are the centerpieces of Minnesota's state flag. The flag is framed with the flowing pink and white lady's slippers (the state flower), a red ribbon bearing the state motto, "L'Etoile du Nord," and the dates 1819 (to honor the establishment of Fort Snelling) and 1893 (to honor the official adoption of the state flag). The year 1858 is centered at the top of the seal, signifying the year Minnesota entered the Union. A white and gold band sporting 19 gold stars (representing the 19 states at the time of Minnesota's admission to the Union) surrounds this centerpiece. The entire design is centered on a royal blue background edged with a gold fringe.

## Other Symbols and Emblems

☛ The elegant pink and white lady's slipper (*Cypripedium reginae*) was named Minnesota's state flower in 1893.

☛ In 1953, the red, or Norway, pine (*Pinus resinosa*—always sure to encourage a chuckle from school children) was adopted as the state tree.

☛ The common loon (*Gavia immer*) was not a lone contender when it came to vying for the honor of being named state bird. The water lover with the ghostly call was up against the American goldfinch, the official club bird of the Minnesota Federation of Women's Clubs. Other suggestions for the title were the blue heron, the veery, the mourning dove, the pile-ated woodpecker, the scarlet tanager, the wood duck and the white-throated sparrow. But on March 13, 1961, the common loon emerged victorious when Governor Elmer L. Anderson signed the legislation making it the official state bird.

☛ The walleye (*Stizostedion vitreum*) was named the state fish in 1965. Incidentally, the largest walleye ever landed in Minnesota weighed 17 pounds, 8 ounces.

☛ The Lake Superior agate is quartz sporting deep red and orange colors. It was named Minnesota's official state gemstone in 1969.

☛ For Minnesota's Native population, it was called "manomin." The wild rice (*Zizania aquatica* or *Zizania palustris*) is prolific in lake areas, and in 1977, it was named the state's official grain.

☛ Do you remember your mom always urging you to drink milk when you were a kid? In Minnesota, drinking milk is not only good for you, it's being loyal to your state. That's because milk was named the official state beverage in 1984.

☛ That same year, the morel (*Morchella esculenta*), a mushroom that looks like a honeycomb, was named Minnesota's official mushroom.

☛ In 1988, the blueberry muffin was named the state muffin—that's right, Minnesotans have a state muffin.

☛ The monarch (*Danaus plexippus*) was named the state's official butterfly in 2000.

☛ Bearing the name "Grace," a photograph of an elderly man, his head bowed in a prayer of thanks for the meal before him, was taken in 1918 by Eric Enstrom and was named Minnesota's official state photograph. It was bestowed with the honor in 2002.

☛ And finally, in 2006, the Honeycrisp apple was named the state fruit.

**DID YOU KNOW?**

The University of Minnesota is one of the leading apple producers and researchers in the world. The crown jewel is of course the Honeycrisp. More than two million trees were planted worldwide in 2006.

# SLEET AND SUN

*Winter is not a season, it's an occupation.*
–Sinclair Lewis

*The coldest winter I ever spent was a summer in Duluth.*
–Mark Twain

*Minnesota might be the only state where you can use your air conditioner and heater—on the same day. With its freeze-your-skin-to-your-clothing winters and sweat-through-your-shirt summers, Minnesota's climate is not for the faint of heart. The weather also has the distinction of being 80 percent of what Minnesotans talk about. The annual growing season ranges from 100 days in the northern counties to about 160 days in southern counties.*

## Average is Good

In a typical year, Minnesotans can expect an average high temperature of 83.4°F and an average low temperature of a moderate –2.9°F.

### Hot Spot

On July 6, 1936, folks in Moorhead were likely drooling at the thought of a long and leisurely swim in one of Minnesota's many lakes or at the very least a cool bath. A record-breaking high temperature of 114°F was recorded that day. It was a record that mirrored an earlier high temperature on July 29, 1917, when Beardsley also saw a high of 114°F.

### Cold Spot

The state's lowest temperature was recorded at Tower on February 2, 1996. The mercury dipped to a nasty –60°F. Locals, used to these cold temperatures, simply refer to the day as February 2.

# Highs and Lows

The community of Lamberton, in Redwood County, experienced the greatest 24-hour temperature change in the state on April 3, 1982. The temperature range between the daytime high and low was a staggering 71°.

# Let it Snow

Average annual snowfall varies considerably from the southern to the northern portion of the state. Folks living in the northeast can expect as much as 70 inches of the white stuff in any given year, while those living in the southwest typically get half that, about 35 inches. Minnesotans can expect at least a couple of blizzards each year. Here are a few interesting snow facts:

☛ The largest snowfall ever experienced in the state during a 24-hour period was 36 inches, which fell near Finland in Lake County on January 7, 1994.

☛ Finland also holds the record for the largest amount of snowfall in a single storm, at 46.5 inches. That record was set January 6 to 8, 1994.

☞ The winter of 1949–50 saw the largest accumulation of snow over one season. A measurement of 170.5 inches was taken that winter near Grand Portage in Cook County.

☞ The earliest official snowfall took place on September 14, 1964, in International Falls, which recorded 0.3 inches of the white stuff.

☞ The latest official snowfall occurred on June 4, 1935, in Mizpah, with 1.5 inches recorded.

DID YOU KNOW?

On October 31, 1991, Minnesota had almost three feet of snow fall on its trick-or-treaters. Ask any resident about the date, and he or she will share stories of children walking through snow-blown paths on the trail to candy.

## Rain Dance

Compared to average annual snowfall, the reverse is true when it comes to average annual rainfall. The southeastern portion of Minnesota gets about 34 inches a year, while the northwest gets about 19 inches a year. What follows are a few more rainy-day figures:

☞ On July 22, 1972, Fort Ripley recorded the largest amount of precipitation in a 24-hour period with 10.84 inches falling that day.

☞ St. Francis recorded the largest amount of rainfall in a single season in 1991. A total of 53.52 inches fell that year.

☞ The driest season occurred in 1976 in Ortonville, with the community recording a paltry 6.37 inches.

☛ The communities of Beardsley, Canby, Marshall and Dawson all have something in common—the longest recorded dry spell in Minnesota history. Between November 9, 1943, and January 26, 1944, not a single snowflake fell.

## Twisted Weather

Although Minnesota is no Kansas, about 18 tornadoes hit the state every year. Seventy-five percent of the tornadoes occur between May and July.

# A Minnesotan's Temperature Converter

Minnesotans use a bit of a different temperature scale than other places. Here is a handy chart for your converting pleasure.

**60 above:** New Jerseyites try to turn on the heat. People in Minnesota plant gardens.

**50 above:** Californians shiver uncontrollably. People in Minnesota sunbathe.

**40 above:** European-made cars won't start. People in Minnesota drive with the windows down.

**32 above:** Distilled water freezes. The water gets thicker in Mille Lacs Lake.

**20 above:** Floridians don coats, thermal underwear, gloves and woolly hats. People in Minnesota throw on a flannel shirt.

**15 above:** Philadelphia landlords finally turn up the heat. People in Minnesota have the last cookout before it gets too cold.

**Zero:** People in Miami start to expire. Minnesotans lick the flagpole.

**20 below:** Iowans fly away to Mexico. People in Minnesota get out their winter coats.

**40 below:** Hollywood disintegrates. Minnesota Girl Scouts are selling cookies door to door.

**60 below:** Polar bears begin to evacuate the Arctic. Minnesota Boy Scouts postpone "winter survival" classes until it gets cold enough.

**80 below:** Mount St. Helens freezes. People in Minnesota rent some videos.

**100 below:** Santa Claus abandons the North Pole. Minnesotans get frustrated because they can't thaw the keg.

**297 below:** Microbial life no longer survives in dairy products. Cows in Minnesota complain about farmers with cold hands.

**460 below:** All atomic motion stops (absolute zero on the Kelvin scale). People in Minnesota start saying, "Cold 'nuff for ya?"

**500 below:** Hell freezes over. The Minnesota Vikings win the Super Bowl.

# WHEN NATURE ATTACKS

*In a place with a climate as relentlessly changing and unforgiving, it is no surprise that Minnesota has its own share of natural disasters. Whether it is flurries in January, floods in April or forest fires in July, Minnesota's climate offers all the hospitality of a wolverine.*

*The National Climate Data Center states that between 1980 and 2006, the United States has collectively faced 70 weather-related disasters that caused $1 billion or more in damage. Here is a sampling of some of the worst to hit Minnesota.*

## Schoolhouse Blizzard

The "schoolhouse blizzard" of 1888 earned its name because its arrival caught many unprepared, including those in one-room schoolhouses. The blizzard was caused by the titanic collision of an Arctic cold front with warm air from the south. Reports from the time indicate the temperature went from 36°F to –20°F (–40°F in some places) in a short period of time. The fast-moving storm first hit Montana, then moved through the Dakotas and, eventually, Minnesota. Because it arrived during working hours and moved in so suddenly, the storm was one of the deadliest ever to hit the Midwest. Historians estimate 236 people died that day.

## The Great Hinckley Fire

The summer of 1894 was unseasonably warm in Minnesota. As the late-summer sun beat down on the woods of north-central Minnesota, no one knew the damage that was about to occur. When you combine record droughts with the then-common practice of lumber harvesting, in which loggers stripped trees of all their branches, littering the ground with debris, you have the recipe for one of the greatest fires in Minnesota history.

The flames started on September 1 and didn't stop for several days. By the time the fire was finally put out, an area of 420 square miles, or 200,000 acres, had been reduced to rubble. The fire decimated the cities of Hinckley, Brook Park and Mission Creek. Scholars are still debating the number of people who died in the blaze, with estimates ranging from 418 to upwards of 800.

DID YOU KNOW?

Boston Corbett, the Union solider who killed John Wilkes Booth, was listed as one of the victims of the Hinckley Fire.

### Armistice Day Blizzard

You would expect a state that doesn't blink at six inches of snow and barely frets over a foot of powder would be ready for anything. However, on November 11, 1940, Mother Nature caught Minnesota off guard. The day started off balmy and pleasant, with temperatures flirting with the mid-60s. However, as the day waned, temperatures dropped like a broken elevator—by afternoon the temperatures had fallen to the 20s and were in the teens by evening. The result was a blizzard that raged like a caged bear. Some parts of the state saw 27 inches of snow over two days. In all, 154 people died, many of them hunters who were not dressed for the weather and were caught unprepared.

# 1918 Cloquet Fire

In the summer of 1918, a fire raged through the northwest corner of the state that surpassed the Great Hinckley Fire. The fire decimated most of Cooke County, devastating Moose Lake, Cloquet and Kettle River. It is the worst natural disaster in the history of the state in terms of the number of lives lost in a single day. In total, 453 people died, 52,000 people were injured or displaced, 38 communities were destroyed, 250,000 acres burned, and $73 million in property damage was suffered.

# Red River Flood

Flooding is unquestionably a way of life when you build a city on the banks of a river. Minnesota's Red River Valley found out how true that is in the spring of 1997. The region had a winter with unusually large snowfalls combined with a spring that pounced with the suddenness of lightning. The resulting flood ravaged everything in its path; land from Winnipeg to Fargo washed away. But nowhere was the damage more severe than in the Grand Forks area. The town's mayor, Pat Owens, ordered the evacuation of 50,000 residents, the largest mass departure since Atlanta was evacuated during the Civil War. The swollen river rushed over the banks and didn't stop until the water reached three miles inside the town, destroying everything in its path.

# LAY OF THE LAND

*From the rugged northern landscape sporting rocky hillsides and pristine lakes to the rolling fields of the pastoral plains, Minnesota is truly a land of diverse beauty.*

## The Big Picture

Minnesota borders the Canadian provinces of Manitoba and Ontario to the north, Lake Superior and Wisconsin to the east, Iowa to the south, and South and North Dakota to the west. Overall, the state occupies an area of 86,943 square miles. Of that, 83,574 square miles are land and 7326 are water. Minnesota is the 12th largest state in the nation.

## Length and Breadth

Travel the state from its southernmost border to where it meets Canada, and you'll cover about 407 miles. The distance from Minnesota's eastern and western borders is a slightly shorter journey at 360 miles.

DID YOU KNOW?

The Arrowhead Region of Minnesota (the top part that sticks out like an apple stem) is the northernmost part of the continental United States.

## Front and Center

Trek about 10 miles southwest of Brainerd, located in Crow Wing County, and you'll find yourself in the geographic center of the state. In case you are interested in the exact coordinates, that would place you at a longitude of 95°19.6' W and latitude of 46°1.5' N. Be sure to bring a boat; these coordinates put you in the middle of a lake.

## High Point

You would typically expect that the high point in a state with a predominantly prairie landscape wouldn't amount to much, even if it does sport the descriptor "mountain" before its name. But Minnesota has a few surprises to offer. At an elevation of 2301 feet above sea level, Cook County's Eagle Mountain offers visitors challenging hiking trails, magnificent waterfalls, roaring rivers and an abundance of wildlife.

DID YOU KNOW?

Aside from Cook County's Eagle Mountain, a lower peak in the state also bears the same name. This second Eagle Mountain is located in the northern part of Minnesota and is home to Lutsen Mountains ski resort. The highest elevation in this area is 1688 feet, almost twice its base elevation of 863 feet.

## Low Point
At 602 feet above sea level, Lake Superior represents the lowest elevation in the state.

## Middle Ground
Minnesota's mean elevation is 1200 feet above sea level.

DID YOU KNOW?

With its large assortment of lakes and rivers, Minnesota has more shoreline than California, Florida and Hawaii combined.

# The Big Ones

Minnesota has 10 major lakes: Upper Red Lake, Lower Red Lake, Lake Superior, Vermillion Lake, Rainy Lake, Mille Lacs Lake, Leech Lake, Winnibigoshish Lake, Lake Pepin and Lake of the Woods (my personal favorite!). Here are a few additional lake facts, courtesy of the Minnesota Department of Natural Resources:

☛ The largest lake in the state, and also the largest inland lake, is Upper and Lower Red Lake, occupying a collective 288,800 acres, or 451 square miles.

☛ Mille Lacs Lake takes second place when it comes to size, occupying 132,516 acres.

☛ At its deepest point, Lake Superior measures 1290 feet.

☛ Portsmouth Mine Pit is the state's deepest inland lake, measuring about 450 feet. The water is so clear you'll swear you can see the bottom.

☛ Cook County's Lake Saganaga is the state's deepest natural lake, measuring 240 feet.

☛ The lake with the longest shoreline is Lake Vermilion. It travels along for 290 miles.

DID YOU  KNOW?

Except for Mower, Olmsted, Pipestone and Rock counties, every county in the state has at least one natural lake.

### Merry Waters
From the moment the calendar flips to December 26, many people officially start counting down to the next Christmas season, so it's good to know that Minnesota keeps the season all year long—at least as far as one of its lakes is concerned. The 257-acre, spring-fed Christmas Lake is located in Minnetonka.

 Boasting 15,291 lakes, Minnesota is truly a water-lover's paradise. But the lakes vary in the creativity of their names. Depending on the source, between 91 and 154 of those lakes share the name Long Lake; 123 are named Rice Lake; and 201 are named Mud Lake. There is also a Mugwump Lake, Dismal Swamp Lake, Ice Cracking Lake, Bologna Lake, Crocodile Lake, Jack the Horse Lake, Full of Fish Lake, Diddle de Woodle Lake and Fun Lake.

### Rivers Run Through It

The Minnesota, Mississippi, Rainy and St. Croix rivers, as well as the Red River of the North represent the state's major waterways. The Mississippi is the longest at 680 miles, followed by the Minnesota at 370 miles. All together, there are about 6564 natural rivers and streams in the state, meandering a total of 69,200 miles.

DID YOU KNOW?

The Mississippi, the Red River of the North and the St. Lawrence all start their journey in Minnesota.

## Wilderness Wonders

For folks who are into the great outdoors, Minnesota's diverse geography offers a vast array of recreational options that include much more than fishing and water sports—though there are ample opportunities for water lovers as well. What follows are a few highlights:

☛ History, wildlife, a 19th-century village, a cave full of icicle-shaped mineral deposits along with an assortment of underground pools await visitors to Forestville Mystery Cave State Park. Located near Preston, the cave itself offers 12 miles of passages. Birdwatchers will enjoy the challenge of identifying many of the 175 bird species reported to inhabit the region at various times of the year. And folks interested in the history of the area's human inhabitants can visit the fully refurbished Forestville townsite. Originally founded in 1853, the community rapidly boomed as a trading center, but when the railroad was built farther south of the town, its demise was just as quick, and by 1890, the entire community was owned by one man, a farmer named Thomas J. Meighen.

☞ The Dalles are river rapids that appear to have carved out a gorge between two steep rock faces. On the Minnesota-Wisconsin border, the Dalles of the St. Croix River tempt avid rock climbers with challenging basalt cliffs.

☞ If you enjoy swimming in your birthday suit, you might want to head down to Hidden Beach. Located on the east side of Minneapolis' Cedar Lake, the beach was once known as "the only nude beach in the Twin Cities." Now known as East Cedar Beach, it's unclear if the practice of swimming in the buff is still common there.

☞ Back in 1882, when maps of Minnesota were first being drawn up, 144 acres of forest were mistakenly mapped as part of Coddington Lake. As a result, the area known as the "Lost Forty," now considered part of the Chippewa National Forest, wasn't logged, and today it boasts some of the state's oldest forests—some of which have red and white pines that measure between 22 and 48 inches in diameter and are estimated to be 350 years old.

☞ If you listen to the powers that be at the National Geographic Society, a visit to Minnesota's Superior National Forest is one of the "1000 places to see before you die." The area, which covers more than 3.5 million acres and includes 2000 lakes and 3400 miles of waterways, is the "eighth most visited forest in the National Forest System." It was first established by President Teddy Roosevelt in 1909.

☞ The natural limestone arch called "In-Yan-Teopa" (Rock with Opening) by the Dakota people is a must-see if you're making your way through Frontenac State Park. The arch is located on a limestone bluff that is 450 feet high and three miles long on the Mississippi. And if your favorite sport is shooting—photographs, that is—Rock with Opening is an impressive example of natural architecture.

☛ *Highways* magazine rated McCarthy Beach State Park as one of the top 17 beaches in the continent to visit, and if you enjoy sandy shorelines and wildlife, you'll likely agree.

☛ Devil's Kettle Falls, located in Judge C.R. Magney State Park on the north shore of Lake Superior, is a natural mystery in its own right. The water tumbling along the Brule River divides in half as it reaches the precipice of the falls. Half the water falls naturally and continues along, while the other half falls into a hole in the earth, and where it disappears to is unknown. One theory is that the water travels through an underground tunnel system that eventually empties into Lake Superior, but this has never been proven.

☛ An oddly shaped rocky wall easily spotted when traveling near Winona wasn't a natural wonder but resulted from an accident of sorts. The wall formed between 1880 and 1887 when the area, now called Sugar Loaf, was mined for its limestone, which was then used in the sidewalks and build-ings of Winona. Interestingly, three other hills near Winona are also named Sugar Loaf.

☛ Big Bog State Recreational Area opened in June 2006, mak-ing it the newest state park. Located north of Waskish Township, swamps and bogs occupy most of the area's 9459 acres.

## Forest Land

There are about 16.7 million acres of forest in Minnesota.

DID YOU KNOW?

There are 58 state forests in Minnesota, covering almost four million acres. The state also boasts 66 state parks, 54 state forest campgrounds, eight waysides, six recreation areas and a state trail.

# CLAIMS TO FAME

*While there are a few traits common to most Minnesotans—
"Minnesota nice," passive-aggressiveness and a love for thermal
underwear—you will find that each community in Minnesota has
its own unique qualities. That's why you should visit each area
individually.*

## County Characteristics

Minnesota is composed of 87 counties. Here are a few interesting tidbits on some of them:

☞ Anoka County derived its name from the Native word meaning "on both sides."

☞ Nine counties border Beltrami County: Lake of the Woods, Koochiching, Itasca, Cass, Hubbard, Clearwater, Pennington, Marshall and Roseau.

☞ With more than 10,000 residents, Sauk Rapids is the largest city in Benton County. But the much smaller city of Foley, with an estimated population in 2003 of just over 2400, is the county seat.

☞ According to the 2000 census, Big Stone County has about 5820 residents.

☞ Blue Earth County was named after the Dakota word *mahkato,* which means "greenish blue earth."

☞ As far as boundaries go, Carlton County has remained as it was at its founding in 1857.

☞ Minnesota's oldest courthouse is the Dodge County Courthouse. It was built out of Mantorville limestone in 1871.

☛ The origins of Koochiching County's name are a bit unclear. "Koochiching" has been translated a number of ways through the years, including "Neighbor Lake and River" by Reverend J.A. Gilfillan, an early traveler through the area, and "A Lake and River Somewhere." White settlers first used the name for the Rainy River Falls and then for the settlement that eventually became International Falls before settling on "Koochiching" as the county name.

☛ As far as area is concerned, St. Louis County is Minnesota's largest, at 6226 square miles. That makes it the largest county in the United States east of the Mississippi River.

☛ Jackson County holds a unique celebration every June called Franks-A-Lot, and boy, do they ever serve up a lot of hot dogs. In 2006, a team of volunteers grilled about 5400 for those in attendance.

☛ The area's Swedish roots are evident in Kanabec County, especially when it comes to outdoor recreation. Each year the county hosts the Vasaloppet—a series of cross-country ski races. The Vasaloppet began in Sweden in 1922 as a commemorative race honoring Gustav Vasa. The young nobleman fled Sweden for Norway on skis when his fellow citizens didn't believe the country was under threat from Denmark. Once they realized the truth of Vasa's warnings, his countrymen struck out on skis to call him back. He returned and led the Swedes to victory against the Danes. In 1972, Sweden gave its blessing to Kanabec County to host an annual Vasaloppet in Mora.

☛ With the motto "Where the Lakes Begin," Kandiyohi County is most definitely cottage country.

☛ Covering an area of about 1,364,480 acres (2132 square miles), Lake County is the fourth largest county in the state. It usually receives about 65 inches of snowfall each year, but during the winter of 1995–96 that number nearly tripled when a record-breaking 171 inches of the white stuff fell.

☛ Lake of the Woods is Minnesota's youngest county. It was formed from the northern portion of Beltrami County and officially came into being on January 1, 1923.

☛ Much of Le Sueur's economy is dependent on agriculture. Statistics from 2002 record 974 operational farms in the county.

☛ It doesn't take a historian to come to the conclusion that Lincoln County was named after Abraham Lincoln, but what is interesting is that the Lincoln County of today wasn't the first to propose that name. Three other attempts at naming part of Minnesota "Lincoln County" were unsuccessful—one in 1861, 1866 and then 1870. Today's Lincoln County was formed in 1873.

☞ Eighty-six percent of Lyon County is designated agricultural land. Overall, the county is divided into 20 townships and boasts 11 cities.

☞ Martin County was once home to about 3000 members of the Ku Klux Klan. Membership in the group grew almost silently in the 1920s, and it wasn't until about 70 prominent members were established in the county seat of Fairmont that anyone even knew of the organization's existence in the state. The Klan's time in the area, however, was short, as residents who once thought it a worthy organization were quickly disillusioned and the group disbanded.

☞ Baby girl Ella W. Hoover gained notoriety the moment of her birth. Not only was she born on New Year's Day 1856, but she was also the first infant born in McLeod County.

☞ While the government of Nobles County wasn't officially up and running until 1870, the county website states the 1861 census reported that 11 families (35 people) lived in the area. Of those, "three were from Norway, three from Bavaria, one from Ireland and the rest from the eastern states."

☞ Agriculture is an important part of Norman County's economy, with soybean production occupying the largest portion of farmland at 173,000 acres. Spring wheat comes a close second with 143,000 acres, and 46,000 acres of sugar beets are a more distant third. These are followed by a smattering of corn, alfalfa hay, sunflower, barley and assorted specialty crops.

☞ Ramsey County is the smallest county in the state, covering just 154 square miles. It's state law that "a city or county with a population of more than 15,000 must annually notify its residents of the positions and base salaries of its three highest-paid employees." As of March 19, 2007, Ramsey County's website identifies those three lucky individuals as a psychiatrist ($151,674), a county administrator ($139,817) and a director of human resource services ($138,769).

☞ One of the oldest sets of Native American remains was discovered near Pelican Rapids in Otter Tail County. Nicknamed "Minnesota Girl," the remains date to about 11,000 BC.

☞ With a population of 1590, according to the 2000 census, Red Lake Falls is the largest of Red Lake County's four cities.

☞ Some of the best private schools in Rice County were said to have been founded by the Right Reverend Henry Whipple of the Episcopal Church. His sensitivity and fair treatment of the area's Natives prompted them to name him "Straight Tongue."

☞ Stearns County is home to Quarry Park. The 643-acre park, with its 20 granite quarries, is considered one of the state's most beautiful parks.

☞ With a population of 19,526 and an area of 423.3 square miles, the population density of Waseca County is about 46 persons per square mile.

☞ Washington County has 62 outdoor warning sirens dispersed throughout the area. The sirens are used to warn residents of extreme weather conditions and are tested once a month between March and October.

☞ Originally, Wilkin County was named Toombs County, after Georgia congressman Robert Toombs. Residents petitioned for a new name, and in 1862, it was changed to Andy Johnson County, after the 17th president of the United States, Andrew Johnson. However, when Congress attempted to impeach Johnson in 1868, residents again petitioned the legislature to change the county name. This time the name Wilkin was chosen, in honor of Civil War hero Colonel Alexander Wilkin.

☞ Winona County was created from part of Fillmore County in 1854, just three years before Minnesota achieved statehood. It is the only county in the state named after a woman.

# Unique Place Names

It is clear that Minnesota's founders had a sense of humor. How else could you explain some of these wacky place names?

☛ Climax holds the distinction of being the only city in Minnesota you couldn't say on TV in the '60s. Word has it that the town rejected the names of Screamer and Raging Orgasm.

☛ Residents of one Minnesota town are real Nimrods. The town of Nimrod sits in Wadena County in northwest Minnesota. It's okay if you haven't heard of it before; the town boasts a mere 75 residents.

☛ If you are having self-esteem problems, you shouldn't visit the town of Embarrass. The town derives its name from the local Embarrass River. The rumor is that the river was so named because it was said to embarrass novice canoeists.

☛ Only the rich soil of the Red River Valley could give birth to a town named Fertile. Located in Polk County, Fertile has a hard time living up to its name—its population of 891 is steadily declining.

*When driving in Minnesota, one must remember that when freeways are labeled North, South, East and West, that doesn't always mean they go that direction. Needless to say, driving can be difficult.*

–Alici, Winnipeg, Canada

# WHAT'S IN A NAME?

*For each interesting place name in Minnesota, there are even more interesting stories about how places were named.*

## Rivals to the End

In the late 1800s, the now defunct town of Manton faced a heated rivalry with nearby La Crosse, Wisconsin. Later, Manton changed its name to La Crescent, the symbol of Islam. The townspeople didn't do this because of a sudden influx of Islamic immigrants; they did it because they assumed (quite mistakenly) that La Crosse was named after the Christian symbol, the cross.

### Well, They Kind of Sound Alike

In 1783, Charles Patterson built a fur trading post. The local Native people grew so enamored with Patterson's bearskin hat that they referred to him as "Sacred Hat Man." Over the years, and losing something in translation, the name of the town became Sacred Heart.

## Bringing Fiction to Life

In southwest Minnesota, a little piece of fiction comes to life. The city of Ivanhoe took its name from the novel of the same name by British author Sir Walter Scott. However, the similarities don't stop at the name—even the streets in Ivanhoe borrow their names from characters in the novel.

## Edina

Although most likely not true, the city of Edina has an interesting story behind its name. Rumor has it that the city's wealthy (er, stuck-up) residents garnered the community the acronym Every Day I Need Attention, thus Edina. In addition, residents of the well-to-do community carry the nickname "cake-eaters."

DID YOU KNOW?

The popular Disney movie *Mighty Ducks* brought the "cake-eater" name to a national level by giving the sweet-toothed moniker to the team's star player, who hails from Edina in the movie.

## Otherwise Known As

The creativity involved in the naming of Minnesota's cities is only surpassed in the nicknames.

Alexandria—Bass Capital of the World

Anoka—Halloween Capital of the World

Austin—Spamtown USA

Barnum—An Arrowhead Egg Basket

Bemidji—Paul Bunyan's Playground; Curling Capital of the USA

Bena—The City Where Partridge Finds Refuge

Brainerd—Hub City

Buhl—Springs of Health

Carlton—Birthplace of the Northern Pacific

Cass Lake—Capital of the Chippewa Nation

Crookston—City with the World's Largest Oxcart

Duluth—Center of the Universe; Unsalted Seas

East Grand Forks—Potato Capital of the World

Ely—City Where Wilderness Begins

Faribault—Athens of the Northwest

Fredenburg—A Pleasant Blend of Progress and Tradition

Gilbert—The Village of Destiny

Hibbing—Town that Moved Overnight

International Falls—Frostbite Falls

Longville—Turtle Center of the World

Minneapolis—City in Touch With Tomorrow; Sawdust City; Mini-Apple

New Ulm—The City of Charm and Tradition

Northfield—City of Cows, Colleges and Contentment

St. Cloud—Nitty Gritty Granite City

Sibley—End of the World

# Sister Cities

In 1955, St. Paul and Nagasaki, Japan, entered into an historic sister city relationship, the first between an American and Asian city. Since then, St. Paul has forged nine new sister city relationships: Changsha, China; Ciudad Romero, El Salvador; Culiacan, Mexico; Hadera and Tiberias, Israel; Lawaaikamp, South Africa; Manzanillo, Mexico; Modena, Italy; Nagasaki, Japan; Neuss, Germany; and Novosibirsk, Russia.

Here are some other notable sister city relationships:

Cambridge—Rättvik, Sweden

Columbia Heights—Mazowieckie, Poland

Duluth—Thunder Bay, Ontario, Canada

Elbow Lake—Flekkefjord, Norway

Minneapolis—Kuopio, Finland

Minneapolis—Santiago, Chile

Moorhead—Druskininkai, Lithuania

New Ulm—Ulm, Germany

Stillwater—Jinja, Uganda

Willwar—Frameries, Hainaut, Belgium

# ALL THE LIVING THINGS

*Minnesota is teeming with plants and wildlife. What's even more special is the biodiversity of the state. The bluffs of the southwest are a completely different ecosystem from the hardwood forests of the north. No matter where you go in the state, you are sure to find something of interest. Here are some of the state's highlights.*

**Where the Red Fern Grows (and lots of other things, too)**
According to the Minnesota Department of Natural Resources, there are 100 fern species in the state, 1600 native flowering plants and 300 non-native, naturalized plants. There is one plant endemic to Minnesota.

DID YOU KNOW?

The only place in the world where you'll find a Minnesota dwarf trout lily (*Erythronium propullans*) growing in the wild is in Minnesota. This makes the name make so much more sense.

## Sky Scrapers

They make them big in Minnesota—trees, that is. There are 52 tree species native to Minnesota. When it comes to tree height, the state is home to three record breakers: a jack pine measuring 56 feet tall and 116 inches in circumference in Lake Bronson State Park; a red (Norway) pine that is 126 feet tall and 120 inches in circumference in Itasca State Park; and a white spruce measuring 130 feet tall and 125 inches in circumference. And anyone visiting the area absolutely must check out the North Shore Witch Tree, which is sacred to the Ojibwa.

## Animal Facts

Minnesota is home to 80 different mammal species. Among the more prolific of the warm-blooded creatures to call this landscape home is the wolf, with a 2004 count of 3020 head. According to the Department of Natural Resources, it's the largest wolf population in the lower 48 states. Of course, this wasn't always the case. From 1849 to 1965, a bounty was offered on the animal. And until May 1974, when the Endangered Species Act put the gray wolf under protection, wolves continued to be hunted and killed under the Directed Predator Control Program. By then, it was estimated that only between 350 and 700 gray wolves still lived in Minnesota.

# Other Populations

The wolf isn't the only animal to fear in Minnesota. Here are some other reasons you should reconsider that next hiking trip:

☞ Between 20,000 and 30,000 black bears live in the state—and they really like to visit campsites for food.

☞ There are approximately 4200 moose that wander throughout the state. Hunting is allowed in some parts of the state, but be careful—moose have been known to use the same logging roads some hunters favor. In an Elmer Fudd situation, occasionally the moose chase hunters!

☞ Cougars (or pumas, or mountain lions), no matter what you call them, are increasingly making their way into more areas of the state. The largest cat in North America, cougars release a scream that sounds not unlike a person being murdered.

☞ Bobcats and lynx roam the northwest corner of the state, and though they are generally afraid of people, you must remember they are still part cat and, as such, hate all humans.

☞ Wolverines aren't common, but any animal that is 50 pounds of muscle, claws and teeth is worth watching out for.

Minnesota may be more civilized than in its earlier days, but in 1929 the folks of Duluth witnessed just how close we are to Mother Nature when a less-than-cuddly, 350-pound black bear moseyed into a downtown restaurant. Although the residents came away unscathed, the same cannot be said for the bear.

## More Cuddly Creatures

☞ The lakes and rivers of northern Minnesota are home to one of the state's most playful animals, the river otter. Tireless travelers, river otters sometimes move up to 25 miles in one day.

☞ Minnesota is home to approximately 1.5 million white-tailed deer. With such a large deer population, each year nearly 14,000 deer collide with cars. In order to control the population, the Minnesota Department of Natural Resources runs a sizeable deer-hunting program. In the late fall, nearly 500,000 hunters head to woods and fields of the state and harvest roughly 200,000 deer.

☞ Gophers, the Minnesota state animal, live throughout the state. Grotesque but well suited to subterranean life, gophers have short legs, huge front feet and claws, large heads with tiny ears, and protruding teeth. Because the critters feed on underground vegetation, they are often unwelcome residents on farms.

☞ The old joke goes "Why did the chicken cross the road?" "To show the raccoon that it could be done." Nowhere is that joke truer than in Minnesota, where "sunbathing" raccoons on the sides of highways are as common as rain in April.

☞ The fox lives up to its trickster billing. Minnesota is home to both red and gray foxes, and both animals can be found in a wide area of the state. As their wild habitat is increasingly turned into housing developments, sightings of foxes are becoming more common in the suburbs.

DID YOU KNOW?

In Minnesota, you can donate your extra deer meat (venison) to homeless shelters.

## Creepy Crawlers

☞ Minnesota is home to several kinds of snakes, with the garter, fox and bullnose (or gopher) snake being the most common. All three species are non-venomous—and relatively harmless— but are good for young boys to use in scaring the fairer sex.

☞ Less common—but more frightening—are the poisonous timber rattlesnake and the massasauga. Both snakes are found in the river bluffs near the Mississippi in southwestern Minnesota.

☞ Although the state harbors numerous species of turtles, easily the coolest and scariest-looking is the snapping turtle. The largest species of turtle in the upper Midwest, the snapping turtle can top 80 pounds in weight and packs a ferocious bite.

☞ The unofficial state bird—the mosquito—is the bane of every Minnesotan's existence. Hatching in late spring—and continuing to annoy throughout the summer—mosquitoes are as welcome as a poke to the eye with a hot stick. On your next summertime visit to Minnesota, make sure to bring loads of bug spray (no DEET, please), and practice your swatting motion.

☞ Despite being small in size, deer ticks pack a lethal punch. Their bites, if left untreated, can be fatal. If you spot a deer tick on your skin, grab the tick with tweezers and slowly remove it. Don't try to burn the bug—it doesn't work, and you will feel dumb when you burn yourself.

DID YOU KNOW?

No one has ever died from snakebite in Minnesota in the last 100 years.

## Flopping Fish

☞ The most sought-after game fish in Minnesota is the walleye. Prized for its sweet, delicate meat, walleye are fished heavily throughout the fishing season. Each year, Minnesota anglers keep roughly 3.5 million walleyes, totaling 4 million pounds. Some of the state's hotspots for walleye include Mille Lacs Lake, Lake of the Woods and the Mississippi River.

☞ Known as "the fish of a thousand casts," the muskellunge (or muskie) is one of the largest and most elusive fish in Minnesota. Its large size allows it to eat other fish and sometimes ducklings and even small muskrats.

☞ Minnesota's largest fish is the lake sturgeon, sometimes weighing more than 300 pounds. Humans can eat the meat, and the eggs are prized for caviar.

☞ With so many lakes, it is no wonder the state is loaded with myriad fish. There are 158 species of fish in the state, residing in 3,800,000 fishable acres of water.

**DID YOU**  **KNOW?**

Minnesota ranks first in the U.S. in fishing licenses per capita.

### Winged Wonders

Of the 428 bird species in the state, about 44 species remain year round. There are about 12,000 common loons, 700 pairs of bald eagles, about 30 breeding pairs of peregrine falcons and more than 1500 trumpeter swans.

# Hidden Treasures

Along with the plethora of plants and wildlife, Minnesota has a bounty of minerals hidden from view. The first shipment of iron ore left the state in 1854. Crushed rock, limestone, quartzite, granite, silica sand, clay and peat are also mined here. And exploration for gold, platinum, copper, nickel, uranium, titanium and diamonds is ongoing. Here's what the mining industry looks like in Minnesota:

☞ nine granite and eight limestone quarries

☞ five clay mines

☞ seven active taconite mining operations in the Mesabi Range

# POPULATING THE PLACE

## Population at a Glance

☛ 5.3 percent of the population claimed to be of foreign birth in the 2000 census

☛ 8.5 percent of the population reported in the 2000 census that they spoke a language other than English at home

☛ 679,236 aged five and older reported having a disability on the 2000 census

According to 2005 census estimates:

☛ 6.4 percent of Minnesota's population were under five years old

☛ 24.0 percent were under 18

☛ 12.1 percent were 65 years and older

☛ 50.4 percent of the population are female

☛ 87.9 percent of residents aged 25 years and older were high school graduates

☛ 27.4 percent of residents aged 25 years and older had earned a bachelor's degree or higher

☛ The average home in Minnesota costs $122,400

MINNESOTA MAGIC

Minnesotans are proud of their heritage. Many cities such as New Ulm, New Prague and Finlayson honor their residents' ancestries with place names reminiscent of their homelands: Germany, the Czech Republic and Finland, respectively.

## Population by Race (2005 Estimates)

| Race | Percentage of Population |
| --- | --- |
| White | 89.6 |
| African American | 4.3 |
| Hispanic | 3.6 |
| Asian | 3.4 |
| Other races | 1.8 |
| American Indian/Alaskan Native | 1.2 |
| Two or more races | 1.5 |
| Native Hawaiian/Pacific Islander | 0.1 |

## Population by Ethnicity (2000 Census)

| Ethnic Background | Percentage of Population |
| --- | --- |
| German | 36.7 |
| Norwegian | 17.3 |
| Irish | 11.2 |
| Swedish | 9.9 |
| English | 6.3 |
| Polish | 4.9 |
| French (except Basque) | 4.1 |

Although those are the main ethnicities represented, Minnesota is starting to see a new kind of immigrant. Drawn by liberal social welfare practices and a strong emphasis on enticing new communities, recent years brought both Hmongs and Somalis to Minnesota's neighborhoods. The majority of Somali immigrants live around the Cedar-Riverside neighborhood in Minneapolis, which now features the largest number of Somalis anywhere outside Somalia. The Hmong people live near St. Paul's eastside neighborhood.

With a total population of 5,167,101, based on 2006 census estimates, Minnesota is the 21st most populated state in the United
States. Its population represents 1.70 percent of the 299,398,484
people who call the country home.

## Population by State

| Ranking | State | Population |
|---------|-------|------------|
| 1 | California | 36,132,147 |
| 2 | Texas | 22,859,968 |
| 3 | New York | 19,227,088 |
| 7 | Ohio | 11,464,042 |
| 10 | New Jersey | 8,717,925 |
| 15 | Indiana | 6,271,973 |
| **21** | **Minnesota** | **5,167,101** |
| 30 | Iowa | 2,966,334 |
| 40 | Maine | 1,321,505 |
| 50 | Washington, DC | 563,523 |

## Population per Square Mile (2000 Estimates)

| State | Population |
|-------|------------|
| New Jersey | 1134.5 |
| Washington, DC | 9378 |
| Massachusetts | 809.8 |
| Ohio | 253.3 |
| Washington | 88.6 |
| **Minnesota** | **61.8** |
| Alaska | 1.1 |

# Minnesota Population through the Years

| Year | Population |
| --- | --- |
| 1850 | 6077 |
| 1900 | 1,751,394 |
| 1960 | 3,413,864 |
| 1970 | 3,806,103 |
| 2000 | 4,919,479 |
| 2006 (estimates) | 5,167,101 |

# Minnesota's Largest Cities

| City | Population |
| --- | --- |
| Minneapolis | 382,618 |
| St. Paul | 287,151 |
| Duluth | 86,918 |
| Rochester | 85,806 |
| Bloomington | 85,172 |

# Minnesota's Most Populated Counties (US Census Bureau 2003 estimates)

| County | Population |
| --- | --- |
| Hennepin | 1,121,035 |
| Ramsey | 506,355 |
| Dakota | 373,311 |
| Anoka | 314,074 |
| Washington | 213,564 |

## Population Fun Facts

☞ About 65,000 children are born in the state each year.

☞ The median age of Minnesotans is 35.4 years.

☞ As of the 2000 census, 17,682 Minnesota grandparents were raising their grandchildren.

☞ Traverse County is the least populated in the state, with 4134 residents.

☞ Of the 384,991 children aged six years and younger, 264,979, or 68.8 percent, have parents who both work outside the home.

☞ The average annual income for a Minnesota family is $56,874.

☞ 7.7 percent of Minnesotans (145,183 people) do not own a vehicle; 590,451 (31.2 percent of the population) own one vehicle; 799,324 (42.2 percent) own two; and 360,169 (19 percent) own three or more.

DID YOU KNOW?

About 84,140 Minnesotans, or 3.3 percent of the population, walk to work. This is likely one of the many reasons why residents of Minnesota are some of the healthiest in the country.

## Minnesota Gem

Treasure is often tucked away in hidden and obscure places, but if you're observant and persistent, you might catch a glimpse of a gem or two. Dorothy Molter was just such a treasure. From 1934, at the age of 27, to her death in 1986, Dorothy lived in the Boundary Waters Canoe area. Initially, she went there as a nurse to care for an aging Bill Berglund, owner of the Isle of Pines Resort. When he died, 14 years after she arrived, Dorothy took over the resort and ran it until 1975. She earned the nickname "Root Beer Lady" because she brewed between 10,000 and 12,000 bottles of the beverage each year. For the more than 7000 annual visitors to the resort, the reception was always warm and the root beer cold.

What remained of Dorothy's homestead after her death was dismantled (it had been earlier condemned by the federal government under the Wilderness Act, but she was allowed to live out her days in her beloved home). It was transported to Ely, rebuilt, and made into the Dorothy Molter Museum in her memory.

## Religious Focus

A survey conducted in 2001 indicated the following preferences among Minnesotans when it comes to choices in religious worship:

| Religion/Denomination | Percentage of Population |
| --- | --- |
| Roman Catholic | 25 |
| Lutheran | 24 |
| No Religion | 14 |
| Other Christian denominations | 13 |
| Baptists | 5 |
| Methodists | 4 |
| Judaism, Islam, Buddhism, Hinduism | 3 |
| Assembly of God | 2 |
| Church of God | 2 |
| Presbyterians | 2 |
| Refused to answer | 6 |

## Baby Names

In 2004, the top five names chosen for baby girls, in ascending order from most to fifth most popular, were Emma, Grace, Olivia, Emily and Abigail. The top five picks for baby boys were Jacob, Ethan, Samuel, Andrew and Tyler.

# ROADSIDE ATTRACTIONS

## Corny Tales

According to area folklore, the considerable foresight that initiated the clearing of land and establishment of prolific corn crops around the town of Backus was the result of the efforts of one Colonel Cobber. And the town has commemorated his memory in two ways—through the carving of a giant ear of corn, which is prominently displayed in town, and the annual Backus Corn Festival, held the second weekend of August.

## Duck!

A statue of a coot—a short-winged, lobed-toe waterbird—graces the roadside of Highway 78 just outside Ashby. The statue was erected to salute Coots Unlimited, the largest men's sport club in the area.

## It'll Rock You

Easter Island has its face-carved stones, England has Stonehenge, and Minnesota has…Blue Mounds. Located in Blue Mounds State Park, it is a line of rocks extending nearly 1300 feet across a hilltop. It is not known who or what placed the rocks, but the structure suggests a human designer. The rising and setting sun lines up perfectly on the rocks at the start of spring and fall.

## Raising Expectations

Canal Park in Duluth is home to the world's largest aerial lift bridge. Viewable from any high point in town (and the hills of Duluth offer many), the aerial bridge is both a boon for tourists and a nuisance for motorists. Any driver unlucky enough to be stuck waiting while the bridge raises and lowers knows it's quicker to melt the winter ice than get across the massive expanse of iron.

Say what you want about "Minnesota nice," Minnesotans are also fantastically proud. The residents of Duluth grew jealous of Superior's (in neighboring Wisconsin) small piece of land extending into Lake Superior. So local Duluth residents did the only logical thing: they built a piece of land that jutted out farther. Not even a court order to stop construction (lawmakers don't look fondly on creating new land, apparently) could slow down the builders. When they received word of an impending injunction, workers labored night and day to finish.

## Earlier Times

The Native American Chief Wenonga is commemorated in statue form on Lake Avenue North in Battle Lake. The statue recognizes the battle that took place in the area in the 1790s. Battle Lake also salutes the memory of the chief in its annual Chief Wenonga Days festival.

## Holy Crow!

Belgrade is home to what's likely the largest crow statue in the world. Sitting on a 25-foot-tall pedestal with the enormous crow perched on a 31-foot-long branch, the monument measures a total of 43 feet in height. The statue is part of the Belgrade Centennial Memorial Park, located on Highway 77 just south of Highway 55. The entire site was built in 1988.

### Ho-Ho-Ho

Folks visiting Blue Earth are greeted by none other than the Jolly Green Giant—the world's largest, or so they claim. Blue Earth also calls itself the "birthplace of the ice cream sandwich" and "home of Minnesota's first stained-glass window."

## Seaside Sculpture

A giant fiberglass serpent guards Serpent Lake and greets visitors to Crosby from its perch at Crosby Park.

# Just Try to Roll It!

It weighs in at 17,400 pounds, is 13 feet in diameter and 11 feet in height—and it is perhaps the greatest evidence yet against evolution. The city of Darwin is home to the "largest sisal (hemp) twine ball built by one person." Securely encased behind glass, the oddity was created by Francis Johnson. According to the visitor's sign, it took Johnson almost 30 years (from 1950 to 1979) to complete his creation. Oddly enough, this isn't the only large ball of its kind. There are three others vying for the title of "world's largest."

## All in the Name

With only about 300 people recorded in the 2000 census, residents of Deer Creek are nothing if not proud of their small community. And they've proven their affinity with a statue of a buck. Apparently it isn't the only Minnesota community to do so. Deerwood and Park Rapids also salute the four-legged creature.

# You Big Chicken, You

Everyone wants to be remembered in one way or another, and Delano's Jon Hanson is memorialized, in a sense, with a giant fiberglass chicken. Hanson, a restaurateur, purchased the statue in 1988 and placed it near his diner, Flippin' Bills. Hanson was known as "Chicken John" for his Friday night legion donations of leftover chicken, and the 13-foot bird seemed like a great gimmick—one that gained him even more notoriety than he'd already achieved after running a restaurant in town for 13 years.

## A Salute to Greatness

Duluth honors the great explorer Leif Erikson with a memorial statue and a replica of the ship he used to sail to America more than 1000 years ago, both located at Leif Erikson Park. The replica ship was built in 1926 and sailed along the same route Leif Erikson initially traveled—all 10,000 miles of it. Once it arrived in Duluth, the ship was purchased by a local resident named Emil Olson and donated to the city. It was then displayed at Leif Erikson Park (formerly Duluth's Lake Park).

# What on Earth is That?

Never let it be said you weren't warned. If you're traveling through Effie and forget to purchase mosquito spray, the giant winged creature near the town's welcome sign should be an instant reminder you might need it. Although Effie is listed as a city, only 91 people were numbered in the 2000 census, so it's unclear if there's a store around where you can purchase the mosquito repellant you'll be looking for. Still, you could straddle the giant mosquito and pose for a photo or two in between slapping the critters silly.

**What a Catch!**
Erskine is living proof that small can be powerful. The community of 437 is home to the Erskine Water Carnival, held every June, and it features the largest northern pike in the world. If you don't believe it, just check out Cameron Lake—that's where a mammoth northern pike statue has been perched for the last 30 years or more. Other big fish statues include a roadside walleye welcoming folks into Isle and another, similar statue, complete with a riding saddle, in Kabetogama.

# Super-Sized Welcome

If you're traveling along Faribault's Wilson Avenue, you can't miss the happy-looking man balancing a giant burger. The statue greets patrons to the A&W Family Restaurant, where you can eat-in or drive-in to enjoy their mighty fine vittles.

**Luring the Big One**
A business in downtown Grand Marais looks a little like it had an accident. Speared through the upper right-hand corner of the building is a walleye that's larger than the big catch of your wildest dreams. It makes for one heck of an endorsement to the product sold in the business housed there. The Beaver House is a family-owned business that sells a wide range of fishing gear, including their trademark live beaver flick lures. If you're an avid fisherman, you'll want to stop by. If you're not, stop by anyhow. The photo will be worth it.

## Slap Shot!

Eveleth is home to the United States Hockey Hall of Fame and calls itself the "Hockey Capital of the United States." It even has a giant hockey stick and puck to prove it. Located in the city's downtown area is a 10,000 pound, 110-foot-long genuine hockey stick built by Sentinel Structures Inc., of Peshtigo, Wisconsin. It's the "world's largest free standing hockey stick" and is listed in *Guinness World Records*. The current stick is the second one to grace the city. The previous version, created by Christian Brothers and authentic right down to the "pro 1000" logo, was erected in 1995. The stick weighed 7000 pounds and measured 107 feet in length. It was replaced with the newer and larger version in 2002.

## More than One

Fergus Falls boasts a few different roadside giants. An otter statue, a Canada goose and a cow all provide visitors with interesting photo opportunities. If you are keeping track at home, that is one giant animal statue for every three residents of the town.

# Look Way Up!

Like every other state in the country, Minnesota has its own collection of statues. Here's where you'll spot a few of them:

☛ Perched near the Hackensack Visitor's Center is a statue of Lucette. According to town lore, the giant woman is none other than Paul Bunyan's sweetheart and wife of 169 years. Really!

☛ Another famous Paul Bunyan statue can be found in Bemidji. He's been standing near the lake with Babe the Blue Ox since 1937.

☛ The "world's largest talking Paul Bunyan" can be found in Brainerd.

☛ Some have claimed Akeley as home of the world's largest statue of Paul Bunyan. The kneeling Bunyan figure measures 25 feet in height, and the statue holds out one hand for folks to sit and pose for family photos. The town is also home to the Paul Bunyan Historical Museum.

☛ A giant lad sporting what appears to be bathing trunks, and who bears no resemblance to Paul Bunyan, stands guard near Hampton.

# Coffee Anyone?

The Swedish influence of early settlers to Lindstrom is evident to even the most cursory visitor. Touted as "America's Little Sweden," Lindstrom has many buildings that reflect Swedish architecture. Karl Oskar Days, a festival honoring the town's Swedish heritage, is held every July. And the community's water tower, erected in 1902, was transformed into the shape of a coffee pot, decorated in Swedish colors and bears the words "Vilkommen Lindstrom."

### Stonehenge with a Difference

An assortment of 21 sculptures of bass instruments are perched on cement pillars and arranged into a bass clef just off Highway 11 near the community of Birchdale. Aptly named Basshenge, the scene draws its inspiration from the circles of Stonehenge, but then takes off in its own direction entirely. The site was the brainchild of a one-time bassist with the Chicago Symphony, Joseph Guastafeste.

## Bronzed Memorials

The community of Hutchinson appears to enjoy remembering its pioneers with bronzed statues—it has a collection of at least four. The first was a statue of the Sioux Native Chief Little Crow, erected in the city in 1937. It was replaced with Little

Crow II in 1982. Ten years later, *Tall Friend, Old Friend* was erected in honor of the city's American Field Service chapter. In 2005, statues of John, Judson and Asa Hutchinson—the city's founders—were erected in Library Square. And most recently, in 2006, a bronze firefighter statue was placed outside the Hutchinson Fire Station. If you're an art lover, all four specimens are well worth the visit.

## History on Display

Residents of Little Falls are mighty proud of their history. Throughout the community are four murals and two frescos commemorating important moments from its past. One mural highlights the town's main street, two others recount the town's logging history in the early 1900s and another shows a little of how the town evolved into what it is today. The frescos can be seen at Lindbergh Elementary School.

### Something Fishy Here!
Folks entering Madison are greeted with more than just a welcome sign. They're welcomed by the town mascot himself, Lou T. Fisk. Sir Fisk is actually a giant codfish—the main ingredient in a traditional Scandinavian dish called lutefisk. And the city professes to be the "Lutefisk Capital of the USA." In case you're curious, lutefisk is prepared by air drying cod and then soaking it in a lye solution for several weeks. At that point, you skin, debone and boil it. What's left has a gelatin-like consistency, and that, my friends, is lutefisk!

## Premium Pizza

With Americans consuming as many as "1.8 billion slices of frozen pizza a year," according to the Red Baron company website, Marshall is proud to be home to a pizza lover's paradise. The Red Baron brand of pizza, produced by the Schwan Food Company, is tossed and topped right in the heart of Marshall. And if you want to know all the ins and outs of how it's done, just stop by the Red Baron Museum.

# Mmm, Mmm, Good!

The folks at Happy Chef Family Restaurant in Mankato are more than happy to dish out their best vittles—and you don't have to go inside to know it. Perched beside the roadside diner is a Happy Chef statue in its full glory, its ear-to-ear grin beckoning hungry travelers as they pass by. At one time, a chain of Happy Chef restaurants, complete with Happy Chef statues, were located throughout the Midwest, but as times changed, tastes changed as well. Today there are still a few Happy Chef restaurants around, but the only one with the smiling chef is the original Mankato location.

### The Shoe Tree Phenomenon Continues

You never really know if these odd roadside attractions will be there from one day to the next, but as of March 2007 you could still see a heavily laden shoe tree over the Washington Avenue pedestrian bridge in Minnesota. So if you're passing by the University of Minnesota, check if it's still there—that is, if you don't have anything more pressing on your agenda! Look closely and you will also see a bike dangling from the branches.

# Amazing Emu

If you're in pain, have a skin condition or are just looking for a nutritional supplement, chances are the folks at the Heart of Minnesota Emu Ranch might have a suggestion or two. Home to about 400 emu, the ranch near Nevis is often considered one of the area's best kept secrets. Along with fresh meat and emu eggs, the ranch sells a variety of emu oils, body creams and other supplements. And if you call ahead, you may be able to book a tour of the 40-acre facility and learn a little more about this amazing bird.

### Hermann Heights Monument

Settlers of mainly German heritage founded the community of New Ulm in 1854. Today, New Ulm refers to itself as "A City of Charm and Tradition," and the celebration of that tradition

can be seen in everything from their annual Visit with
St. Nicholas to Hermann the German, a statue erected in 1890
to celebrate the hero of the ancient German Battle of the
Teutoburg Forest. No one knows much about the real
Hermann; historians aren't even sure if Hermann existed or is
just folklore. New Ulm is also home to the musical, 45-foot-tall
Glockenspiel Clock Tower.

## Celebrating Snow

If you can't beat it, join it—the weather, that is. Snow is no
stranger to St. Paul, and every year the city celebrates Sno-Daze,
a festival that brings the youngster out in just about everyone.
In an effort to get into the spirit, every winter, the North
St. Paul Jaycees build a giant snowman at the corner of
Highway 36 and Margaret Street. But after a few lean winters,
snow-wise that is, the group decided to erect a permanent snowman of the white stucco variety. The statue is so important to
the community that plans to enlarge a local highway had to be
altered so as to not interfere with the colossal stuccoman.

## Regal in Redwood

Towering 25 feet high, a voyageur statue watches over Pine City.
The statue salutes the city's early days as an area trading post
and was carved out of redwood by chainsaw artist Dennis
Roghair. It sits just off old Highway 61.

## Witches Hat

Rising from the hill on Prospect Park is a tower known as
Witches Hat. The tower is the subject of numerous local legends. One of the most famous is that Bob Dylan wrote the song
"All Along the Watchtower" there while ditching classes at the
nearby University of Minnesota.

## Vacation Destination

Pipestone calls itself "Home of the Red Stone Pipe," but there are a few other interesting tidbits it's famous for. It is home to the historic pipestone quarries, about 800 wind generator towers and the natural rock formation called the "Old Stone Face."

## Roadside Art

Vining is a tiny city with a population of just 68 residents, according to the 2000 census, but it has a whole lot of big things to see. Artist Ken Nyberg has created several sculptures, among which are a giant foot, a potted cactus, half a watermelon being sliced by a giant knife, a pair of pliers ready to squash a bug and a cup pouring coffee.

# YOU GOTTA SEE THIS!

## Shop Till You Drop

Shopaholics will love this must-see destination. Bloomington is home to the Mall of America, "one of the most visited tourist destinations in the world," and the largest mall in the United States (second largest in the world). The mall first opened its doors in 1992. Along with 520 stores, 50 restaurants, assorted attractions and ongoing events, the mall offers patrons 20,000 free parking spots. Get out that credit card! There are plans to enlarge the structure, finally claiming the title of "world's largest mall."

The Mall of America covers 9.5 million square feet—the size of 78 football fields. If you were to spend 10 minutes in every store at the mall, it would take you more than 86 hours to complete your visit. Now that's a lot of shopping!

### History in Stone

Harmony is home to the Niagara Cave, one of the largest natural caves in the Midwest, and visitors can expect a breathtaking hour-long tour that can't be duplicated anywhere else. Among the cave's many features are a waterfall that towers 60 feet high, large icicle-shaped mineral deposits called stalactites, fossils dating back 400 million years and even an underground wedding chapel, where at least 300 couples have tied the knot. Following the tour, visitors are encouraged to mine for their own gemstones and fossils or, if they prefer, pick out one or two of their favorite varieties at the gift shop. And a picnic site provides visitors with a restful space for lunch before carrying on. This one is not to be missed!

## Colorful Collector

If you tend to purge your excess belongings, you should thank your lucky stars you weren't married to Edwin Krueger of Wykoff. Oh, he was a likeable enough character. It's just that from the time his wife died in 1940 to his death in 1989, he lived a bachelor's life and, well, he tended to collect things. Actually, he collected and kept *everything*—from matchbook covers to his dead cat (appropriately placed in a neatly labeled shoebox, of course). When he passed away, he willed that his little Jack Sprat Food Store (where he lived and accumulated his collection) be turned into a museum. Obviously, even death couldn't make the beloved eccentric throw anything away!

# Vince Shute Wildlife Sanctuary

Tucked away in the woods of northern Minnesota, near the town of Orr, is a 360-acre wildlife sanctuary with a special concern—bears. About 80 black bears call this haven home at varying times of the year, and thousands of visitors take advantage of safe viewing areas to observe the bears in their natural habitat. While bears had been visiting the area for many years, Vince Shute formally donated the land and established the American Bear Association in 1995. As well as the bears, the sanctuary hosts all manner of wildlife, from timber wolves and white-tailed deer to bald eagles and blue jays.

### Thanksgiving Came Early

Those lucky enough to be driving through Frazee on the afternoon of July 1, 1998, were treated to the largest roasted turkey ever. The town, famous for producing turkeys, featured a giant fiberglass turkey mascot, dubbed "Big Tom" by the residents. However, the beloved mascot went up in flames during the July heat. In what can only be chalked up to marvelous foresight, the town had already ordered a replacement turkey. Something seems fowl here...

### Ancient Mysteries

Spelunking enthusiasts should try to stop by Forestville some day. The city is home to the Forestville/Mystery Cave State Park. Underground visitors get a tour of the cave, complete with underground pools and unique mineral formations. And if you're a tad claustrophobic, you can wait above ground and check out the restored historic village, circa 1800.

# Jewel of the North

Rochester was recently named "Best Small City" in the nation by *Money* magazine, and it's something the city is mighty proud of. One of the city's proudest attractions is the Mayo Clinic—widely considered the top hospital in the world.

## Ellsworth Rock Gardens

If you're the adventurous sort and don't mind boarding a boat to get to your destination, a visit to the Ellsworth Rock Gardens is well worth the effort. Located on the Kabetogama Peninsula, in Voyager National Park, is a rock garden complete with an array of rock sculptures created by Jack Ellsworth. Over 20 years, from the 1940s to the 1960s, Ellsworth crafted the rock creations and surrounding flowerbeds that continue to draw visitors throughout the summer.

# You Callin' Me a Quack?

Minneapolis is home to a one-of-a-kind museum—or at least a museum that houses the largest collection of a particular set of artifacts. The Museum of Questionable Medical Devices, also known as the Museum of Quackery, has been the focus of curator and founder Bob McCoy's life for as long as he can remember. The unique collection includes all sorts of weird and horrific devices, such as a Vibratory Chair (1900) used to lose weight and a shoe-fitting x-ray device. McCoy has written about his collection in a book called *QUACK! Tales of Medical Fraud.* The museum is now housed in the Science Museum of Minnesota.

# This Old Farm and More

Take a trip down memory lane with a tour of Paul Bunyan Land and This Old Farm Pioneer Village. Located on State Highway 18 just outside Brainerd, the farm offers "50 acres of history and future" in a reconstructed pioneering village complete with barns, dental and doctors' offices, a fire station, gas station, blacksmith shop, church, school and a giant clock modeled on Paul Bunyan's pocket watch and so much more. Each scene takes visitors back to the early 1900s and is complete with antique tools and gadgets from the period being represented. The entire site is a labor of love that was started by Richard Rademacher and continued by four generations of the

Rademacher family. The museum claims to be "the largest one-man collection in central Minnesota." The farm also offers visitors a professionally designed corn maze, carnival rides, games, events and more.

**Answered Prayer**
The summer of 1876 looked promising to the folks farming the countryside surrounding Cold Spring. Mother Nature was cooperating with the perfect mix of sun and rain, and the rich earth seemed anxious to produce. Within 24 hours that all changed as a swarm of grasshoppers, not unlike the biblical plague of locusts, consumed everything in sight. To make matters worse, the grasshoppers left behind their eggs, threatening a repeat performance the following year. On April 26, 1877, the state governor proclaimed a day of prayer. Reverend Leo Winter of the Order of St. Benedict led area residents in a marathon prayer session, promising the Blessed Virgin that if she'd rid the area of the pesky insects, they'd erect a chapel in her honor. The legend goes that the grasshoppers disappeared the next day, and as promised, a chapel was constructed on Chapel Hill—a grassy knoll midway between the church in Jacobs Prairie and the St. Nicolas mission. A tornado destroyed the church in 1894, and it wasn't until 1951 that another was built in its place, this time with donated granite. Today, Assumption Chapel remains a must-stop for visitors and residents alike.

DID YOU KNOW?

Grand Rapids boasts the largest pumpkin patch in northern Minnesota. The plethora of squash are located in Nordic Ridge Gardens, and the public is invited to come down from the last week in September to the end of October to check out the more than 20 varieties, as well as take part in some good old-fashioned fun that includes a five-acre corn maze.

## Fantasy Wonderland

If you're traveling near Kellogg with a car full of youngsters, you might want to plan a stop at LARK Toys. The company, whose name stands for Lost Arts Revival by Kreofsky, has been manufacturing wooden and tin toys since 1983. And although they pride themselves on recapturing the magic of yesterday's toys, there's nothing old fashioned about their business savvy. The factory covers 31,500 square feet, and aside from an area used to create and sell their toys, LARK Toys provides patrons and their tots with a carnival-like experience. Children can enjoy a ride on a handmade carousel, peruse books, have a bite to eat or take a trip down memory lane at the Moose Tracks Museum, which houses thousands of toys from the 1900s to 1960s.

## Hobnobbing with the Hobos

Starbuck sits on the shores of the state's 13th largest lake, Lake Minnewaska, and folks wanting to camp out in the area can do so at the city's Hobo Park Campground. Of course, a giant hobo mascot, nestled in beside the campground's welcome sign, greets visitors from the beginning of May to the end of September. The campground offers boat docks, a public beach, and hikers and cyclists will enjoy trails at the nearby Glacial Lakes State Park. One thing that's not clear, however, is why it's called Hobo Park. Hmm?

## Angler Alert!

If you can't imagine a holiday without a fishing pole and tackle box, then Nevis is the destination for you. Literally hundreds of lakes are almost within casting distance of the town, but be prepared! In very short order, you could be hauling in the walleye, bass, panfish or muskie of your dreams! And in case you have any doubt, the town has erected what it calls the "World's Largest Tiger Muskie" on the east end of Lake Belle Taine.

## Pharmacy Facts

You'll learn everything you ever wanted to know about the prescription drug industry if you stop by the William & Joan Soderlund Pharmacy Museum in downtown St. Peter's. Sponsored by Soderlund Village Drug, the museum covers everything from the history of drugstores in the country to the evolution of the industry. And if you aren't in that neck of the woods but are still interested, check out their online museum.

# Waterfront Warrior

There's no doubt that Two Harbors has a long list of interesting things for families to see and do, but perhaps the most unique, as far as the Minnesota landscape goes, is the Split Rock Lighthouse. The story goes that a harsh November gale in 1905 resulted in a number of shipwrecks in the area, prompting the U.S. Lighthouse Service to construct a lighthouse. It was completed in 1910 and is touted as "one of Minnesota's best known landmarks." Visitors can tour the lighthouse and then check out the visitor center to get information or to pick up a souvenir or two. Just a little trek away, near Agate Bay, is the Lighthouse Point and Harbor Museum. This lighthouse was erected to aid in the transportation of iron ore from the area. It is the only operating lighthouse remaining in the state.

# SMALL TOWN ODDITIES

## The Name Game

The story of how Nowthen got its name isn't likely duplicated anywhere in the world. Apparently James Hare, the town's postmaster back in 1897, suggested several names for the community where he'd just set up shop. Before signing his name to the document with his suggestions, he added "nowthen" and, as fate would have it, that's the name the Post Office Department chose.

## Spam-a-Lot

The Hormel Corporation, located in Austin, is the largest independent meat and food processor in the United States. For all the respect heaped on the company, it is ironic that they are perhaps most well known for producing one of the least respected meats: SPAM. Disturbingly pink and smelling vaguely of formaldehyde, SPAM is the subject of numerous jokes and urban legends. The Hormel Corporation lists SPAM's official ingredients as chopped pork shoulder meat with ham meat added, together with salt, water, sugar and sodium nitrite to help preserve color.

### Celebrating SPAM

Who knew Austin was home to the SPAM Museum? According to the museum, everyone should. In a salute to SPAM lovers everywhere, the museum is an astounding 16,500 square feet of SPAM-related stuff. After all, SPAM is "the cradle of civilization...the ultimate culinary perfection." A visit will arm you with an understanding of the development of the canned meat, its role during World War II, SPAM advertising campaigns throughout the years, SPAM trivia and more! Open since 2001, organizers promise "1000 percent fun."

## A Meal in a Can

Hormel Corporation's other contribution to the food landscape is Dinty Moore stew, which originated during the Great Depression. The Hormel Corporation canned meat and potatoes in round tins for distribution to those less fortunate. However, the program ended before Hormel could use up all their tins. As a result, the Hormel Corporation began to sell a canned stew and called it Dinty Moore. The rest, as they say, is eating history.

DID YOU  KNOW?

Hawaii, of all places, is the largest consumer of SPAM of any state.

TOURISM AND TRAVEL

# The Big Catch?

It's not exactly like dining in the belly of a whale, but it's pretty close. Folks traveling along U.S. Highway 2, northeast of Bena, might find themselves doing a double take as they pass the town's Big Fish. The Big Fish Supper Club welcomes diners with its renowned, 65-foot-long, 14-foot-high muskie. When the muskie was first built in 1958, it housed a hamburger joint, but today the supper club is located in the adjacent building. The fish is pretty famous, though. It appeared in the movie *Grumpy Old Men*.

# Out of This World!

Speaking of unique dining options, Minnesota boasts three Space Aliens Grill & Bar restaurants—one located in Waite Park (the first franchise to the original restaurants opened in May 2003), Albertville (opened in April 2006) and the other in Blaine (opened in early 2007). According to Internet reviews, the restaurant plays up the theme of an alien encounter to the hilt. Scenes from outer space are painted on the domed ceiling, alien sculptures abound and galaxy games occupy youngsters (of all ages) in the attached arcade.

### Mo-ooose

Karlstad, population 900 and counting, calls itself the "Moose Capital of the North." Folks there are so darn proud of their four-legged, furry friends that they've erected a moose statue and host an annual Moose Fest.

# Butter it Up!

The city of Olivia claims to be the "Corn Capital of the World." Their motto is "Grow with us!" They have a 25-foot-tall cob of corn welcoming visitors and residents alike. Their corny mascot Cornelius is a favorite among parade-goers, and anyone who attends the community's Corn Capital Days is provided with a free corn and bean feed.

76

## A Glorious Place to Poop

Well before Thomas Crapper invented the modern bathroom (yes, someone named Crapper invented the crapper), outhouses were the preferred method for answering nature's call. One of the most decadent outhouses is in Belle Plaine. The outhouse is two stories tall and is attached to the Hooper-Bowler House. Visitors to Belle Plaine can even purchase shirts proclaiming the tiny town as "Home of the Two-Story Outhouse." And who wouldn't want to own that sh**...I mean shirt...

DID YOU  KNOW?

International Falls calls itself the "Icebox of the Nation." If you've been there, you would say "icebox" is an understatement.

## Small Town, Big Heart

Every community likes to boast of their assets, and Menahga is a small town with a lot to boast about! Named after the Native word for blueberry, which typically grows in pine forests, Menahga comes by its slogan "Gateway to the Pines" quite honestly. The town is also proud of its friendly disposition, calls itself a "four-seasons vacationland" and is known as the "Home of St. Urho." And what do you do when your country lacks a quotable saint the likes of St. Patrick? You invent one—or at least the story. One creative Minnesota resident named Richard Mattson devised the story of St. Urho (a real saint) and how he saved Finland's grape crop from poisonous frogs. Although not nearly as cool as St. Patrick ridding Ireland of snakes, Mattson's version also suffers from the lack of poisonous frogs in Finland and a total absence of grape crops. Never mind. The town of Menahga built a St. Urho statue, but changed the frogs to (slightly) more believable grasshoppers.

# The Big Screen

Wabasha was the scene for two major motion pictures—*Grumpy Old Men* in 1993 and its sequel, *Grumpier Old Men,* in 1995. The town is also set to be the future home of the National Eagle Center.

# RECORD BREAKERS AND FIRSTS

## A Lone Eagle

The first man to cross the Atlantic in an airplane hailed from a farm near Little Falls. Charles Lindbergh Jr. won a $25,000 prize for being the first to cross the pond in a solo, nonstop airplane flight from Long Island, NY, to Paris, France, in 1927.

### Keeping in Shape

If you're a cross-country ski enthusiast, travel on to Grand Marais and then a little farther north, and you'll find the longest set of trails in Minnesota. The site boasts 150-miles worth.

## Ancient Relics

Visit Minnesota's River Valley and you'll see some of the oldest rocks on earth, dating back 3.8 billion years.

### Standing Tall

In a salute to miners in the iron ore industry, an 81-foot-tall Iron Man statue greets visitors to Chisholm—"The Heart of the Iron Range." It's believed to be the third tallest free-standing statue in the country.

### Education Firsts

Minnesota's first college was Hamline College (later known as Hamline University). It opened its doors in 1854. The institution also led the way in the fight for equal rights between men and women as one of the first colleges in the country to offer co-ed classes.

DID YOU KNOW?

The Christian brothers of Warroad founded the company that makes Christian Brothers hockey sticks. Roger and Bill Christian were 1960 U.S. Olympic gold medalists, and the brothers followed up on that success by creating their company in 1964. Their motto is "Hockey sticks by hockey players."

## Makin' the Ladies Happy

Although some folks call the Southdale Center in Edina the first shopping mall in the world, it's more correctly "one of the first." Sources credit the Country Club Plaza, built in 1924 in Kansas City, Missouri, as the first of its kind. The Edina mall can, however, take the claim as being the first enclosed shopping mall in the United States. Who would want to shop outside anyway?

### Two of a Kind

Brainerd and Pipestone are the only two communities in Minnesota to have concrete water towers.

## Child-Centered

The Minneapolis Public Library is thought to have been the first to establish a special children's section. The library separated children's books from the rest of the collection in December 1889.

### Encore! Encore!

Since first opening its doors in 1940, the Old Log Theatre in Minneapolis has entertained more than six million people.

## Brrrum, Brrrum

If they knew, children everywhere would be grateful to the Mound Metalcraft Company. The fledgling manufacturer, back in 1949, operated out of a schoolhouse basement and produced the first TONKA toy trucks. With their operations set up near Lake Minnetonka, it's no big mystery where the brand name came from.

### Everyone Loves Chocolate
Mars, Milky Way, Snickers, Three Musketeers—what these chocolate bars all have in common is their inventor, Frank C. Mars. He was born in Newport, Minnesota, on September 24, 1883.

### Open Wide
Minnesota is home to the largest operating open-pit mine in the world. The Hull Rust Mahoning Mine measures in excess of three miles in length, two miles in width and 535 feet in depth. It's nicknamed the "Grand Canyon of the North" and was the first of its kind on the Mesabi Iron Range. The Mesabi Iron Range spans parts of Itasca and St. Louis counties. It is the largest iron ore deposit in the nation.

## Wild and Wonderful

In 2007, the Eloise Butler Wildflower Garden and Bird Sanctuary celebrated its 100th birthday, and if all the enthusiasm surrounding the place is any indication, it'll likely be around for at least another 100 years! Located on Theodore Wirth Parkway and Glenwood Avenue in Minneapolis, the 15-acre garden is the largest of its kind in the entire nation. Park staff estimate about 60,000 visitors tour the facility each year.

# Ecology Conscience

Minnesota leads the country when it comes to making changes to save the environment. In 2005, the state became the first to legislate that all diesel fuel sold in Minnesota must be at least 2 percent biodiesel—fuel made from soybean and other vegetable oils. It only makes sense, considering that the previous December, Minnesota opened its first biodiesel plant near Redwood Falls.

DID YOU  KNOW?

The concept of opening a Dead Letter Office came about in 1825 as a way to deal with undeliverable mail. Apparently there are three such offices in the United States—one in Atlanta, Georgia; one in San Francisco, California; and one in St. Paul, Minnesota. Interestingly, items collected at the Dead Letter Office are offered for auction.

## A Fisherman's Paradise

The Lutsen Resort and Sea Villas have extended hospitality to visitors for more than 100 years. The family-owned business first opened its doors to the public in the late 1800s and doesn't show signs of slowing down. It's believed to be the oldest resort in the state.

# The World of Religion

Whether it's a rare, one-of-a-kind volume of ancient theology or something far less obscure, chances are Loome Theological Booksellers can find what you're looking for. The bookshop, which is located in a restored convent church in Stillwater, calls itself the "largest secondhand dealer of theological books in the world." With as many as 275,000 volumes lining the walls, it's hard to argue otherwise!

### Business the Bailey Way

According to the 2000 census, the population of Newport sits at around 3715 residents. Although not the largest community in the state, it is home to one of the country's largest and longest operating wholesale nurseries. For four generations, and for more than 100 years, the Bailey family has operated Bailey Nurseries, providing 4500 businesses with first-rate trees, shrubs and other nursery products.

# Last Survivor

Albert Henry Woolson was recognized as the "last surviving member of the Union Army." He died in Duluth in 1956 and at that time was believed to be 109 years old. However, records discovered after his death put him at 106. Either way, he definitely enjoyed a long life.

**DID YOU KNOW?**

The Tilt-A-Whirl carnival ride is a Minnesota creation. It was an idea developed by Herbert Sellner of Fairbault back in 1926.

# FESTIVALS

*Minnesotans love their fairs and festivals. On any given summer evening, chances are there is a local or community celebration near you. Residents and visitors use these celebrations to relax, socialize and, of course, drink.*

## The Great Minnesota Get-together

With more than one million visitors over 10 days, the Minnesota State Fair is the largest state fair in the nation. The fair features vendors from all over the state, as well as any food you can imagine that can fit on a stick. In recent years, some creative foods such as spaghetti, macaroni and cheese, and deep-fried candy bars found their way onto sticks. But not all things at the fair are fried—there is beer, too. Each night a different national act plays the grandstand to an audience filled up on food and fun times. With over 100,000 visitors a day, the fair offers some of the best people-watching one could hope for.

## The Winter Carnival

Minnesotan's have their own twist on the saying "When life hands you lemons, make lemonade." In these parts, they say "When life hands you ice, make a friggin' huge castle."

Minnesota's Winter Carnival started in 1885 when a visiting journalist from (prissy) New York proclaimed the city "Another Siberia, unfit for habitation." In an effort to prove their where-withal in regard to the cold, city officials decided to build a giant ice castle. Montreal was planning on building one of their own, but a smallpox epidemic killed (forgive the pun) those hopes. Minnesota, ever the opportunist, stole the architects from the Montreal team and brought them to Minnesota. Using ice from a local lake, they built a castle 106 feet high. Despite temperatures of –20°F (take that, Siberia!), residents lined up by the thousands. The Winter Carnival has been an annual tradition ever since 1885, making what Minnesotans call "the coolest celebration on earth" the oldest and largest winter festival in the country.

**DID YOU  KNOW?**

F. Scott Fitzgerald's story *The Ice Palace* centers around Minnesota's penchant for ice-block architecture.

### Festival Quashed

Folks in Gilbert don't consider themselves hard to get along with. They enjoy a party just as much as the next person. And initially, in 2005, when a group of businessmen thought of hosting an annual festival that would promote their city's history and set their town apart from any other community festival in the state—or even the country—residents were all ears. But when organizers started laying out detailed plans, the initial enthusiasm turned into outrage. And what did these entrepreneurs think they'd call the proposed annual festival? Whorehouse Days. The festival's aim was to celebrate the community's early history when it was known as the "red-light district of the Iron Range." Needless to say, the proposed festival never got off the ground.

## Slow and Steady

Every Wednesday, beginning the first Wednesday of June and lasting until the end of August, the town of Nisswa hosts the Nisswa Turtle Races. It's a tradition that has spanned 40 years and doesn't show any signs of slowing down…so to speak. And if you don't own a turtle, don't worry. On-site vendors have a variety of critters for you to choose from.

## Celebrating Friendship

The rest of the nation may not be aware, but there's a little bit of Canada in the heart of Minnesota. Little Canada is a suburb of the Twin Cities metropolitan area. Because the area had a fair contingent of residents with French Canadian roots, it seemed a natural idea to celebrate the U.S. bicentennial with its nearest neighbors to the north, the residents of Thunder Bay, Ontario. That first festival took place in 1976. Since then, the two communities, now sister cities, gather in Little Canada for the annual Canadian Days festival every August. Along with the food vendors, beer gardens, midway rides, parades and endless entertainment, Canadian dignitaries are warmly welcomed and Canadian Days pins are handed out to anyone who wants one! Talk about international friendships.

# HAUNTINGS

## The Hangman's Noose

The last man hanged in Minnesota is believed to haunt the state to this day. He wasn't a nice fellow, but you can't help but feel just a tiny bit sympathetic to his cause. In 1913, William Williams was sentenced to death after being found guilty of sexually assaulting and murdering a young boy. However, the young executioner was inexperienced and didn't account for the stretch in the rope, or the stretch of the neck, and Williams hung a full 16 minutes, his toes sweeping the floor, before the hangman grabbed his body, pulled with all his might and broke Williams' neck. The staff lunchroom of the St. Paul's Ramsey County Courthouse was built on the site, and Williams' ghostly image has been seen dropping from the ceiling from time to time.

### A Matter of Principle

Despite being condemned to death for the murder of her elderly husband, Ann Bilansky obviously did not approve of the Catholic Church's decision to leave her grave at St. Paul's Cavalry Cemetery unmarked. From her death in 1860, her black-cloaked form was frequently seen wandering about as if looking for her nonexistent headstone. In 1940, a headstone was finally put on her grave, and her wandering spirit hasn't been seen since.

## Museum Madness

This story will have you thinking twice before checking out another museum. It's believed that a portion of the Minneapolis Institute of the Arts known as Area 35 is haunted by the spirits of individuals who once owned the period furnishings housed there. Visitors have reported feeling ill when walking through the area. And some former staff members have reported encounters with ghostly apparitions.

## Struggling Students

Everyone knows college students are poor. Add to that an end-less stream of bills that need to be paid and worry over grades and where to get their next meal, and stress levels run high. But for a few students who opted to move out of their school dormitory to share a house on Winona's 362 Cummings Street, life was even more stressful. Shortly after moving there, the students realized they had at least one other tenant—and he wasn't of the earthly variety. A shadowy figure was seen in bedrooms, outside windows and throughout the house by a number of the students. But the icing on the cake happened during a party when the house was cleared by a noisy clanging in the furnace.

# Creepy Civic Center

Folks in Minneapolis believe their city hall has been haunted since March 18, 1898, the day convicted thief and murderer John Moshik was hanged. The botched execution, which really amounted to Moshik being hanged twice and likely choking on his own vomit, took place on the fifth floor. On three separate occasions, legal representatives fell ill after entering what had been the courthouse where Moshik was convicted—one judge recovered, one died and a lawyer passed away from a heart attack. These and other occurrences must have been convincing enough, because in 2001 the historical society hired the Minnesota Paranormal Investigative Group to look into the matter.

## Routine Walk-Through

St. Paul's Calvary Cemetery has been used, from time to time, as a training ground for potential investigators with the Minnesota Paranormal Study Group. It was just such a situation that brought folks out to the area between 9:30 and 10:30 PM on September 30, 2006. On entering the cemetery, the lead investigator felt as though the group had "walked into a party and the music stops and everyone is looking at you like you have your pants around your ankles." Sounds like the newbie got her fair share of otherworldly experiences that night!

# Stage Presence

Mantorville's Opera House is believed to be haunted by at least two spirits, according to the Minnesota Ghost Hunter's Society—but that's not a surprise to the people who frequent the establishment. Permitted to investigate the premises, the ghost hunters discovered that a woman named Ellen, whom patrons have heard playing with the stage electronics from time to time, is definitely an entity inhabiting the place. The opera house also offers an unknown male spirit; however, he seems to be relegated to the basement only.

## Mystic Museum

Glensheen Mansion, in Duluth, has a lot going for it. Not only is it among the most beautiful, stately historic houses in the country, but its 100-year-old walls have also been transformed into a porthole to the past. Operated by the University of Minnesota, the mansion is a museum, taking visitors on a journey through the area's history. Some folks have claimed to get more than a museum tour, however. The talk around town for some time now is that the mansion is haunted, and investigators from Mystical Blaze seem to agree. Although staff members are instructed not to discuss the matter, the mansion was the scene of a grisly double murder in 1977. The mansion's owner, 88-year-old Elizabeth Congdon, and nurse Velma Pietila were the victims, and originally Elizabeth's husband was convicted of the crime. He was acquitted five years later. Elizabeth's adopted daughter Marjorie was also suspected of committing the deed, but she was also acquitted. To date, no one has been punished for the brutal crime. No wonder the place is haunted!

# Lonely Spirits

The spirit of a young boy killed by an arrow through the eye is believed to haunt a hillside in Apple Valley. Reports of toboggans being pushed into trees and woeful moaning sounds are quite common, but most believe the ghostly presence is merely lonely and looking for a playmate.

## Yummy!

The Old Broadway Food & Spirits restaurant in Alexandria might serve up a mighty fine meal, but the building's history is anything but appetizing. Apparently the building was once a brothel and morgue, though it's unclear if it served both these purposes simultaneously. Ghostly apparitions have been reported by patrons and staff, among them the image of an old woman, who, most believe, is actually quite friendly.

# Love Triangle

Haunted restaurants aren't unusual, or so it seems, and Forepaugh's Restaurant in St. Paul is just one more example. The eatery is located in an historic, 1870s Victorian-style mansion once owned by Joseph Lybrandt Forepaugh. One story tells of how Joseph became involved with one of his servants, an affair that abruptly ended when his wife Mary discovered the two in a rather compromising situation. The servant, now pregnant, was horribly distraught at losing her lover and hanged herself. Joseph attempted to go on with his life, but in 1892, he, too, committed suicide, though some suggest that business concerns rather than the loss of his lover was the propelling factor in this tragedy.

The mansion was sold several times before the current owner purchased it in 1983 and turned it into a wonderful fine-dining restaurant. The food is said to be marvelous, but every once in a while, patrons report seeing an attractive man strolling through the premises "as if he owns the place." Imagine that.

*One of my favorite traits of a typical Minnesotan is our genuine hospitality and conversational style. We take forever to say goodbye—we always have something else to mention, a story to tell or more 'hot dish' to send home with you.*

–Laura, Faribault

# GHOST TOWNS

## New Prairie

In its heyday, about 21 residents lived in New Prairie. According to sources, the town was open for business from about 1912 to 1954. Of course, changes in transportation routes often affect the future of a place, and when the railroad stopped making deliveries to New Prairie, the population dwindled even further. If you drive by today, you might see the remnants of an old store, but that's about it.

### Belle River

In the mid-1860s, Douglas County was home to the community of Belle River. Among the first buildings erected in the area was St. Nicholas Catholic Church in 1871. Eventually businesses set up shop, along with a post office, and by the end of the century, it seemed as though Belle River had a promising future. But in 1906, the post office closed, which is always a bad sign as far as the state of a community goes, and in 1915, a fire destroyed the church. It was replaced the following year by a gothic-style, red-brick church that seats as many as 800 parishioners. Although the church is still in use, the town's population has dwindled. Most folks have moved away, and the buildings that remain are mostly rubble.

## Clayton

The community of Clayton seems to have suffered the boom-and-bust cycle of many others of its day. Jacob Shirk was the area's first settler, arriving in 1856 and establishing the community of Prattsville. It was renamed Clayton in 1860 when the post office opened its doors for business. Soon after, a church, creamery, homes and assorted other businesses were built in the area. But by 1899, the church shut its doors (which is definitely a bad omen), along with the post office and blacksmith shop. Shortly thereafter, the businesses and school closed down. Today, all that remains is the local cemetery and one house.

# Pomme de Terre

Established in 1868, the first village in Grant County was that of Pomme de Terre. In less than 40 years, it boasted not one, but two general stores, several shops, an elevator, hotel, school and more. In 1873, the community was in the bidding for the position of county seat. But when that didn't happen, and the railroad decided to lay its track farther north, the community began to dwindle. What was once a townsite is now part of a private farm, and all that remains of Pomme de Terre is the old schoolhouse and cemetery.

# Shell City

Wadena County's Shell City is little more than a shadow of its previous self. Originally founded in 1880, Shell City was once a thriving community. If you visit the site, you'll still notice the hard-packed earth where wagon trains once traveled, and one source states that as many as 100 wagons made up a single caravan. The positioning of the railroad also led to the demise of this community, and aside from the wagon trails, all that's left are a few building foundations and a cemetery.

# STRANGE AND BIG THINGS

## It's a Plane. No, it's a Bird!

Pelican Rapids claims to have the "mother of all pelicans." The 15.5-foot-tall statue was built in 1957 and is located on the Pelican River, which flows right through the downtown area.

### Historic Graffiti

It's a mystery to city officials and historians alike, but the south wall of 123 South Broadway in Crookston is covered in notes and messages dating back to the 1890s. The names, dates and short messages—such as that of Slim Berg who notes he's "heading south" and dates his entry "June 9, 1918"—were obviously meant for an audience of some kind, but no one seems to know why or when the practice started. One source suggests the building was centrally located from the hotel, depot and other public amenities and served as a message board of sorts. Some folks carved their messages into the soft stone, while others used pencil. Either way, this unique piece of history offers a brief insight into the lives of residents and visitors throughout the decades.

## When Buildings Become Art

Architect Frank Gehry—of phallic fish fame—vowed not to create "another brick lump." Instead, he created a giant steel dump. Gehry's undoubtedly more famous creation, the Guggenheim Museum in Spain, is often considered an architectural triumph, but his Weisman Museum on the University of Minnesota Twin Cities campus doesn't garner the same praise. Some refer to the tin structure—which predates the Guggenheim by four years—as a blight on the city's horizon; others say *really* mean things.

# Uniquely Urban

If you live and work in Minneapolis' downtown core, chances are you can get yourself to work and home again, pick up groceries on the way, and maybe even dine out without ever stepping foot outside. The reason? The city has a unique skyway system that travels about five miles throughout the city. Couple that with the downtown's many enclosed walkways, and you can handle whatever challenges Mother Nature, or anyone else for that matter, throws at you.

# ASSORTED WEIRDNESS

## Butter Me Up!

Butter sculptures aren't a new idea for folks attending the Minnesota State Fair. As early as 1898, butter sculptures have been featured—it was a unique way of advertising the state's claim as the "Butter Capital of the Nation." But in 1965, Linda Christensen came up with a unique idea. To honor the dairy princess, "Princess Kay and the Milky Way," and the 11 other contestants named each year at the fair, she used a 90-pound block of grade "A" butter to recreate each likeness. The result was so amazing and was such a big hit with the crowds that she continues to make sculptures of each contestant.

## Garden of Delight

Ask anyone what his vision of Minneapolis is, and after he says "cold," he will probably talk about "the big spoon with a cherry." Designers Claes Oldenburg and the impossibly awesomely named Coosjie van Bruggen constructed their artistic vision in the Minneapolis Sculpture Gardens. The garden has been around for a long time in one form or another, originally opening as Armory Gardens in 1913. But today, after several renovations to neighboring buildings, along with expansions and redesign of the garden itself, rotating art displays and a name change to the Minneapolis Sculpture Gardens, the site is thought to be the largest urban sculpture park in the country. Also of note in the garden is Frank Gehry's fish jumping from a fountain. Go ahead, try to say it doesn't look phallic.

# NATIVES TO NOW

*The history of Minnesota is shaped by its original Native American residents, by European exploration and settlement and by the emergence of industries made possible by the state's natural resources.*

## Who Says Cavemen Were Dumb?

The ancient people who lived around Lake Superior were the first in North America to make metal tools. Archeologists have evidence of tools dating back 5000 years.

Archaeological evidence of Native American settlements dates back to 2000 BC. The Jeffers Petroglyphs in southwest Minnesota feature illustrations believed to be nearly 3000 years old. Around 700 BC, burial mounds were first created. There are several places in the state where you can visit these ancient mounds. Indigenous cultures continued to spread throughout the state with the addition of Hopewell and Mississippian cultures.

DID YOU KNOW?

In addition to the "Minnesota Girl," another set of early human remains found in Minnesota dates back almost 9000 years. The man, dubbed "Brown's Valley Man" because he was found near Brown's Valley, was discovered in 1933. Some of the earliest evidence of a sustained presence in the area comes from a site known as "Bradbury Brook" near Mille Lacs Lake. The site, used around 7500 BC, was part of a vast trading route in the area.

### Rewriting History

If it's the real deal, a 36-x-16-inch slab of Graywacke stone could hold the key to mysteries of an unknown medieval civilization. Discovered in 1898 by a Minnesota farmer named Olaf Öhman, the tablet is valuable because of the runic writings on its surface that apparently tell of a Norwegian and Goth exploration into the area in 1362. Named the Kensington Runestone, it is still being studied but can be viewed by the general public at the Runestone Museum in Alexandria.

The runestone has spurned controversy among Swedes, Italians and Norwegians. If the stone is authentic, that means Vikings—not Columbus—were the first to "discover" America—and they did so long before the Italian Columbus set foot on American soil.

## What the Runestone Says

The text on the runestone, written in ancient Swedish, says:

8 Geats (South Swedes) and 22 Norwegians on acquisition venture from Vindland far to the west. We had traps by 2 shelters one day's travel to the north from this stone. We were fishing one day. After we came home found 10 men red with blood and dead. AVM (Ave Maria) Deliver from evils.

## On the Move

The Kensington Runestone's early history reads like a comedy. Once discovered, the stone was displayed in a local bank. An error-laden copy of the stone made it to the University of Minnesota, where a professor of Greek—yes, Greek—declared it a forgery. Olaus J. Breda, a professor of Scandinavian languages and literature at the university, also declared the stone a fake. However, no one realized that Breda, though he was Swedish, was not familiar with runic script.

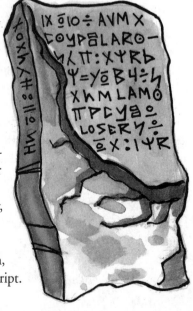

As well, Norwegian archaeologist Oluf Rygh concluded the stone was a fraud. Rygh, a close friend of Breda, never actually saw the stone (or any inscriptions) and, you guessed it, he knew nothing about runes.

With scholars either dismissing it as a prank or unable to identify a credible historical context, the stone was returned to Öhman, who is said to have placed it facedown near the door of his granary as a "stepping stone," which he also used for straightening out nails. Öhman's son, trying to relieve fears that the stone had been mistreated, said it was simply thrown into their barn.

The stone has changed hands more often than a fruitcake over the last 100 years. In recent years, archeologists have used more modern tools to date the stone, with each test producing conflicting results.

## Evidence for the Runestone

☞ During this time in history, it would be possible to travel from Scandinavia to North America without ever crossing more than 200 miles of open sea (but traveling over lots of ice would be no less difficult).

☞ In 1354, King Magnus Eriksson issued a "passport" for Paul Knutson to check on the Swedish settlement in Greenland. Knutson found the area abandoned, apart from some extremely cold and lonely cattle. It is believed the former settlement rejected the church, decided to go on a southern vacation and trekked to North America.

☞ Historian Gustav Storm documented the journey, suggesting the voyagers returned in 1363 or 1364.

☞ A letter dated 1577 from Gerard Mercator to John Dee describes a voyage beyond Greenland. His letter says eight men returned to Sweden in 1364.

☞ Although no copy of a book called *Inventio Fortunate* remains, the book is cited by a number of other scholars of that era and is believed to have been an account of the journey. Some maps list *Inventio* as a source for their depiction of the Arctic and northern North America.

☞ The runestone was believed to have been found under a poplar tree, with the tree's roots wrapped around the stone. The actual tree was destroyed, but several nearby poplars of the same size were cut down. By counting their rings, it was determined the trees were 40 years old, thus suggesting the original poplar was around 30 years old at the time of the discovery. Since the surrounding county had not been settled until 1858, it is unlikely the trees roots could have had the time to grow around the stone.

☞ The words etched on the stone can almost be traced back to other texts of the time. It is unlikely that the people in North America had the knowledge or ability to re-create these symbols.

## Why the Runestone Could Be a Hoax

☞ The runestone's discovery by a Swedish farmer in Minnesota at a time when Viking history and Scandinavian culture were such popular—and controversial—topics is problematic.

☞ Why a man who is being chased by ravenous Natives and fearing for his life would take the time to carve his story on a large stone is confusing.

☞ It is difficult to imagine why there is little to no evidence of other Viking settlements from Nova Scotia (the likely landing place) on down to Minnesota until much later in history.

☞ Some scholars note a discrepancy between the symbols on the tablet and other symbols normally used at the time.

# A Less Controversial Story

It is hard to say who discovered Minnesota (that would be like saying Al Gore discovered the Internet), but no one debates that the French turned up in droves in the 1650s. They were lured by the pristine land, endless expanses and highly sought-after furs. The first Europeans there included the impossibly French-sounding Medard Chouart des Groseilliers and Pierre-Esprit Radisson. In 1659, Frenchmen Jacques Marquette and Louis Joliet discovered the northern portion of arguably the most important waterway in North America, the Mississippi River.

The Natives and French settlers lived in uneasy balance until 1680, when the Dakota captured Rene Robert Cavalier and Sieur de La Salle. To be fair, the men had entered Dakota Territory. Eventually they were released, but the practice of capturing French settlers continued. In 1683, the geographically challenged Catholic missionary Father Louis Hennepin returned to France after exploring Minnesota. After being held captive by the Dakota, Hennepin wrote the first book about Minnesota, *Description de la Louisiane.*

For the next 100 or so years, the Natives were too busy fighting with one another to notice that the European powers were playing poker with their native lands. In what can only be called the greatest "trade" in history, Spain received the Louisiana Territory (including what is now Minnesota west of the Mississippi River) from France in compensation for its loss of Florida during the Seven Years War. Great Britain won claim to what is now eastern North America (east of the Mississippi River) and Canada. The Natives, as you can guess, were not factored into the decision.

DID YOU  KNOW?

The only portion of Minnesota that featured British soldiers during the American Revolution was Grand Portage, along Lake

Superior. The lack of soldiers here can be attributed to the lack of any revolutionaries with which to quarrel.

## The Story Continues...

Spain, like a child tired with its toys, re-gifted the Louisiana Territory back to France in 1800. Once again, the number of Natives consulted on this decision was zero. In 1803, the United States bought the Louisiana Territory from the French. If you are keeping score at home, that means France owned the area twice, Spain and the United States once, and the Natives awaited yet another change of hands.

The United States governed the area until the War of 1812. The Natives, sensing a chance to give the proverbial finger to the bastard Americans, supported the British—if for no other reason than they had never used their land for Christmas presents.

In 1836, the Wisconsin Treaty was drawn up and incorporated a good portion of Minnesota. This wasn't terribly important until 1841, when Wisconsin entered the Union as a state, leaving residents of the area between the Mississippi and St. Croix rivers (current-day eastern Minnesota) without a territorial government or legal system.

## Can the Dakotas Play, Too?

Throughout the first half of the 19th century, what is now called Minnesota faced an identity crisis. The northeastern portion of the state was a part of the Northwest Territory, then the Illinois Territory, then the Michigan Territory and finally the Wisconsin Territory. The western and southern areas of the state were not formally organized until 1838, when they became part of the Iowa Territory.

The newly founded Minnesota Territory was formed in 1849. The population amounted to fewer than 4000 people, not including persons of pure Native American heritage—as the U.S.

government had already made it quite clear that persons of pure Native American heritage did not matter, at least not in censuses.

DID YOU  KNOW?

The first Minnesota paper was the *Minneapolis Pioneer.*

 The population of Minnesota began to boom between 1853 and 1857 as more settlers discovered what millions know today: Minnesota is awesome. The population soared from 40,000 to 150,000 during that time, with most residents residing in St. Paul, St. Anthony and Stillwater. People came to the area to participate in the booming lumber and fur trading industries.

### A State At Last

On May 11, 1858, Minnesota realized its grand ambition of achieving statehood. It was the 32nd state admitted to the Union. Minnesota began a host of firsts, which includes holding the first state fair and naming the first governor, Henry Sibley.

## Fortifying the State

Starting in 1800, Minnesota set about building what was then called Fort Saint Anthony. Situated at the convergence of the Mississippi and Minnesota rivers, the fort was an ideal place to defend the region's fur traders. Later renamed Fort Snelling— after Colonel Josiah Snelling, the original commander—the fort was used for troop training during the Civil War. Snelling is credited with personally negotiating disputes between Native tribes in the area.

Fort Snelling even played a role in the Dred Scott Decision— the monumental Supreme Court case on slave representation. Scott was in service at the fort until his master moved back to

Missouri. When his master died, Scott sued for his freedom, citing his time spent in service in Minnesota (a free state).

The fort was used throughout World War II to teach soldiers Japanese. Today the fort features reenactments and lots of airplanes. The Minneapolis-St. Paul airport is close enough that you can smell the exhaust.

### Pierre "Pig's Eye" Parrant

The city of St. Paul owes its existence to Fort Snelling. A group of squatters, mostly from Selkirk Colony in what is present-day Manitoba, established a camp near the fort. The squatters were deemed to be too close to the important fort, and the commander forced the squatters downriver. Pierre "Pig's Eye" Parrant moved his mod squad and established a saloon, becoming the first European resident in the area that later became St. Paul. The squatters named their settlement "Pig's Eye," after Parrant. The city that Pig's Eye founded was later named Lambert's Landing and then finally St. Paul.

While much mystery surrounds Pig's Eye's life, one thing is for sure: he has, without a doubt, the coolest name of any city founder in Minnesota history. The name "Pig's Eye" lives on as a beer in the area—popular with local college kids, the brew is uncommonly cheap and hangover inducing.

The earliest name for St. Paul comes from a Native colony *Im-in-i-ja Ska*, meaning "white rock," and refers to the limestone bluffs nearby.

## Troubling Times

The excitement of statehood was tempered quickly by the outbreak of the Civil War in 1861. Minnesota initially sent 1000 servicemen to fight for the Union Army. Casualties were abundant—at the Battle of Gettysburg, the First Minnesota

Regiment lost 215 of 262 men—but the state continued to send troops. By the time the war ended in 1865, Minnesota had sent 24,000 men to serve in the Civil War, or Indian Outbreak.

Also around this time, Minnesota was involved with what was known as the Dakota Conflict. Enraged by the failure of land treaties and mistreatment by the Minnesota government, Chief Little Crow led a group that attacked white settlers at the Lower Sioux Agency. The initial attack led to satellite attacks around the state. By the end of the conflict, 486 white settlers had died—and untold numbers of Natives lost their lives.

As a result of the attacks, 39 Native people, whom it was decided committed the most egregious crimes, were sentenced to death by hanging. President Lincoln reduced the original number of 303, as he distinguished between those who had engaged in warfare against the United States and those who had committed the crimes of rape or murder of civilians. On December 26, 1862, 39 Native Americans were hanged in Mankato. It was, and still is, the largest government-sponsored execution in the nation's history. Lincoln later said that it was one of the saddest and most troubling times of his life.

After the attacks, Minnesota declared all treaties with the Sioux void—though it could be argued they would have done this anyway. Most shocking, all Sioux were expelled from the state. In 1863, the scalp of a Sioux was worth $25. Although this was one of the state's darkest times, stories abound of Sioux aiding the settlers and settlers aiding the Sioux.

DID YOU KNOW?

Minnesota's State capitol was completed in 1905 by world-renowned architect Cass Gilbert. Gilbert used as his example the capitol building in Washington, DC.

# FOUNDING FATHERS

## James J. Hill

It's not a stretch to say that Hill was one of the most important business people in the history of the United States. Starting in railroads and branching off into other areas, Hill was a true giant of industry. He was bestowed with the moniker the "Empire Builder," a name he lived up to again and again. Hill successfully navigated through numerous downturns in the economy and overcame every law meant to slow him down. Not even the powerful Teddy Roosevelt and his trust-busting measures could slow down this freight train of a man. At the time of Hill's death, he was worth over $53 million—well over a billion dollars in today's money. Hill's legacy lives on at the James J. Hill House and the James J. Hill Reference Library, which is considered the premier library for practical business information in the United States.

## Pierre-Espirit Radisson

Perhaps the first European recorded in the Minnesota history books, Radisson explored the northeast section of the state along Lake Superior. Radisson, along with his brother-in-law, Medard des Groseilliers, was a prominent fur trader in the area. His legacy is still evident in the Minneapolis-based hotel chain, Radisson Hotels.

## Henry Wadsworth Longfellow

There is no indication he ever set foot in the state, but Longfellow has as much to do with Minnesota's rise to prominence as any-one. His epic poem "The Song of Hiawatha" is based on stories of local Natives and first put Minnesota on the map.

## Henry Hastings Sibley

The first governor of the state, Sibley rose to prominence while serving as a Justice of the Peace in the Iowa Territory. In the first election, he ran against another prominent Minnesotan, Alexander Ramsey.

# OUT AND ABOUT

## Something for All Seasons

Minnesotans love to get out and experience the great outdoors. No matter the season, they find a way to make the best of the weather. In spring, many Minnesotans dust off their fishing boats and head for the water. As the temperature rises and spring moves to summer, Minnesotans take advantage of the numerous walking, hiking and running trails. Whether you want to relax on the beach or water ski, the many area lakes offer endless summertime opportunities. With the arrival of cooler temperatures and beautiful leaves of fall, Minnesotans turn their attention to hiking and the start of hunting season. The subzero temperatures of winter provide the necessary ice and snow for ice-fishing, hockey, snowmobiling and cross-country skiing.

With one boat for every six residents, Minnesota ranks first in the nation in boat ownership per capita.

## Blaze Orange: The New Fashion Statement

Each November, nearly 500,000 Minnesotans don their best in blaze orange and make their yearly pilgrimage to the woods. In Minnesota, deer hunting isn't reserved for just the men; it is a whole family sport. Over the 15-day season, hunters will bag nearly 200,000 deer. Deer hunting is such an event in some communities that schools and workplaces see a sharp drop in attendance. Some communities even go so far as to declare the first couple days a holiday, allowing students and workers to commune with nature without the guilt!

One unique aspect of Minnesota lifestyle is having a family cabin. Many families own a lake house to use on the weekends. With the immense popularity, lakeshore real estate has skyrocketed in recent years, with some of the more desirable parcels of land increasing their value tenfold.

# EATING AND PARTYING

## Eat Street

In a state that features so many ethnic cultures, it makes sense that there is great diversity in food offerings. The headquarters of the Minnesota ethnic culinary scene is an area known as Eat Street in Minneapolis. Stretching for 16 blocks from Grant to 29th Avenue, the area is so popular that it has its own website. The site claims that "Diverse and delicious, it's where east meets west, north meets south and the Upper Midwest gets a good chile relleno, Szechwan wonton, spanakopita or wiener schnitzel." It's possible to have a Greek appetizer, a Brazilian steak and an Ethiopian dessert without ever leaving the block.

## Global Market

If Eat Street isn't your scene, check out the new Midtown Global Market. Located in the old Sears building in Midtown, the market offers authentic food from around the world. In addition to the food, there are numerous stores that offer products from a variety of cultures. So if you want a kebab from Kabul and a dejimbe from Djibouti, the Midtown Global Market is the place to go.

## When It's Time to Party

If Eat Street is the headquarters of Minnesota's food scene, then the Historic Warehouse District is the place for those looking to imbibe spirits. Named because many of the bars are converted warehouses from Minneapolis's flour-milling days, the district has as many options as it does cocktails. Whether you are looking for a top 40 dance club, Irish pub, cocktail lounge, strip club or college hangout, the Historic Warehouse District has what you need. But beware—on Fridays and Saturdays, the area can get wilder than your uncle at the family holiday party.

## Fresh From the Farm

In a state where farming thrives, it should come as no surprise that Minnesota is home to numerous farmers' markets. When summer hits, farmers bring their wares to these markets where the public eats the food up...literally. The food offered varies according to the time of year and location, but whatever you choose is guaranteed to be delicious; Minnesota's farmland is some of the most productive in the nation. So, on your next summer visit, make sure you check out the local farmers' market and see what is in season.

## Apple Picking

If you missed the summer farmers' markets but still want farm-fresh goods, just head to the local apple orchard. Despite the cold winters, Minnesota is one of the top apple producers in the country. In fact, because of the high quality of their apples, Minnesota apple growers receive the fifth highest price in the nation for their apples. Notable varieties of apples developed in the state include Harleson, Fireside, Honeygold, Regent, Honeycrisp and next in line, Zestar! If you aren't interested in apples, fret not; most orchards offer hayrides, corn mazes, pumpkin patches and all other manner of fall festivities.

There are more than two million Honeycrisp trees growing around the world. From Seattle to Germany, Honeycrisp apples are growing wherever you can find a cool climate. The Honeycrisp is so popular that it was voted one of the "25 Innovations that Changed the World" by the Association of University Technology Managers. The tasty treat came in just behind advances such as the Google search engine and electronic hearing implants for the deaf.

DID YOU KNOW?

The University of Minnesota's fruit-breeding program is the only program of its kind in the Midwest, and one of only four in the nation. Since its inception, the program has produced more than 100 cold-weather varieties of fruit such as currants, blueberries, raspberries and, of course, apples.

## No One Does It Like Grandma

Everyone knows grandma's is the place to go for food—but also for drinks? Over the past 30 years, Grandma's Bar and Grill has been serving up food and drink to the visitors of Duluth. Named after Grandma Rosa, the company's website claims the original Grandma first opened her boarding house to hungry sailors on the shores of Lake Superior in the late 19th century. The boarding house closed, but the restaurant still serves up meals to sailors, tourists and residents alike. Today, Grandma's restaurants are known as much for their over-the-top décor and sassy attitude as for their food. Since opening the original store in 1976, Grandma's has expanded their operation to include nine restaurants in Minnesota. In addition, the restaurant sponsors the Grandma's Marathon in Duluth, a race run by nearly 10,000 participants each year.

LIFESTYLE

# LEARNING THE LINGO

## The Way We Talk

Despite what many may think, people in Minnesota don't speak like the characters in *Fargo*. That said, there is definitely a local vernacular to learn if you want to converse with a Minnesotan. A popular book entitled *How to Talk Minnesotan: A Visitor's Guide* by Howard Mohr instructs readers how to talk with a Minnesotan and function in the passive-aggressive Minnesota culture. Mohr highlights such gems as how to ask for seconds (turn down the host three times, then accept on the fourth offering) and how to wave.

Here are some other highlights that well help you talk with the next Minnesotan you meet:

**The Beach:** Contrary to popular belief, Minnesotans don't need an ocean to go to the beach. Any body of water with land around it is perfectly acceptable for beach activities.

**Black Ice:** Scarier than seeing your parents naked, black ice is feared by every Minnesota driver. It results when emissions freeze on the road (yes, it does get that cold in Minnesota), thus creating an invisible sheet of ice.

**Brat:** No, not an unruly child, but bratwurst. It is like a really big hot dog that snaps when you bite it. Best when cooked in beer and festooned with mustard and sauerkraut.

**Cabin:** A second dwelling that nearly all Minnesotans possess. Usually situated on a lake, cabins need not be ornate—just provide a venue for fishing and beer drinking.

**The Cities:** The Twin Cities metropolitan area and surrounding suburbs. It is commonly believed to extend from Forest Lake in the north to Lakeville in the south, and from Stillwater in the east to Burnsville in the south. Say "the cities" to any Minnesotan, and they will know instantly what you are talking about.

**Dinkytown:** A small grouping of hippie coffee shops, bars and bookstores located next to the University of Minnesota. Sightings of white males in dreadlocks are not uncommon.

**Duck, Duck, Grey Duck:** The proper way to say the children's game that involves kids running around and hitting one another on the head. If you say "goose" in Minnesota, be ready for a finger to touch you in an inappropriate spot.

**Hockey:** One of two things that might be occurring when you see large numbers of Minnesotans gathered outside in the winter (see Ice Fishing for the other). It is a commonly held belief that God created hockey and made Minnesotans the best at it because he wanted his people to be happy.

**Hot Dish:** What lesser-educated people refer to as a casserole. Hot dish is commonly served by women with graying hair at church get-togethers and family dinners. Recipes vary, but all must include green beans cooked to different consistencies.

**Ice Dam:** A serious problem all Minnesota homeowners dread. Say "ice dam" to any Minnesotan, and you will see the person run and grab a tool that resembles a giant razor. Ice dams result when snow melts, and then, five minutes later, freezes in a different spot (usually in the least convenient spot on the roof).

**Ice Fishing:** The other outdoor option for Minnesotans in the winter. Minnesotans love fishing in freezing weather, so much so that they invented their own pole for it that looks not unlike what a child learning to fish might use.

**Ice House:** No, it's not cheap, hangover-inducing beer, but the place where Minnesotans go when their cabin is closed for winter. Any structure used to keep hearty fisher people warm

when it is –36°F. Structures range from shower curtains to elaborate buildings worthy of Hollywood royalty.

**Lutheran:** The good side.

**Nope:** The only acceptable response when you don't agree.

**Out East:** Anything east of the Mississippi.

**Pop:** What others mistakenly call "soda." I don't know why it is called pop, it just is.

**Rambler:** A one-level house found everywhere in Minnesota

**Real Doozy:** A descriptive adjective used to add extra emphasis to a situation—usually weather related, as in "That blizzard was a real doozy."

**Snow Day:** The subject of every Minnesota schoolchild's prayers. In order for a snow day to occur, two of the following four things must happen: a temperature of at least –38°F, three feet of snow, the earth falling off its axis or a governor's pardon. Snow days in these parts are rarer than Bigfoot.

**Tar-Jay:** Not the name of a drug, nor a limb-swinging pal of Tarzan, "Tar-zhay" is the Minnesota-ized pronunciation of the Minnesota-born retailer, Target.

**Warming House:** A must in winter where any outdoor hockey rink is located. It warms you up as you lace up your skates or after you are finished skating. It usually smells like a stew of hot sweat or a dead skunk (which is not a bad thing).

**Uff Da:** An interjection used when you have faced a harrowing day or nearly injured yourself, as in "Wow, what a day. Uff da, I am tired."

**Up North:** An adjective used to describe the location of most Minnesotans on summer weekends, the location of which can be anywhere north of Anoka.

**Ya:** The way to agree with someone, usually said twice. "Ya" can be followed with "you betcha" if you live north of St. Cloud.

**Yep:** An acceptable substitute to "ya." Take care to place extra emphasis on the "p" sound.

*I've noticed that here in Minnesota, there is a lot of nodding. Having spent much of my childhood in Tulsa, Oklahoma, nodding of the head was not something I was accustomed to. And I've never been able to figure out exactly what all the nodding means. It's not always as agreeable as one might think. Someone can nod the entire time I'm talking, and then completely disagree with everything I've said. So far, I've been able to deduce that all the head nodding is akin to saying something like, 'As a fellow human being, I respect your right to speak.' If you're from Minnesota, you may want to check whether or not you've just nodded along with everything I've written.*

*–Sarah, Tulsa, Oklahoma*

# DRUGS, BOOZE AND ALL THINGS INDULGENT

## High Times

The state's close proximity to Canada makes Minnesota a thoroughfare for drug trafficking, with marijuana and meth being the most common drugs on the street. In recent years Minnesota has undergone a major crackdown on the use of meth.

### I Don't Think We're in Hollywood Anymore

Located in Center City, the Hazelden Clinic is the go-to place for Hollywood stars with drug or alcohol problems. The center has never released its client records, but public record indicates that celebrities from Eric Clapton and Melanie Griffith to Chris Farley and Owen Wilson have "camped" at Hazelden.

## The Best Brewpub in the Land

If you find yourself thirsty while visiting Duluth, make sure to stop in at Fitger's Brewery. Just on the edge of town, Fitger's Inn and Brewery complex offers almost anything a weary traveler could hope for. Make sure to test some home-brewed suds at the brewpub—the state's largest—and take a tour of the facilities. If you are serious about your beer, this is the place to go—Fitger's offers over 100 handcrafted beers throughout the course of the year.

DID YOU  KNOW?

Gluek, Hamm's Schmidt, Schell's, Grain Belt, Cold Spring and Stroh's served their first golden suds in Minnesota.

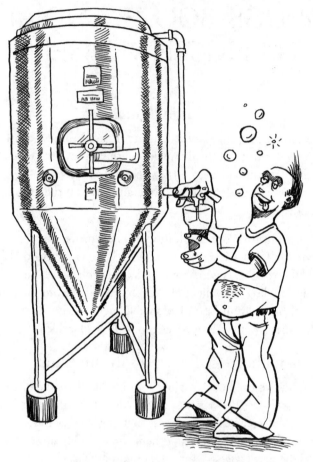

## Brewing Up a Storm

What do you get when you combine agricultural people and winters so cold you don't dare go outside? Breweries. Lots of breweries. At one point Minnesota boasted 167 breweries. Those nasty years known as Prohibition and heavy competition reduced that number, but Minnesota still has enough breweries and beer pubs to indulge your beer tooth. As you travel the state, ask any local where to get the best beer and he or she will be happy to point you to an inviting pub with fresh-brewed suds.

 The Schmidt's brewery in downtown St. Paul used to have a giant sign that illuminated the beer's name at night. Legend has it that two locals, who grew tired of what they believed to be watered-down beer, scaled the walls and removed several key letters (C, M, D and the second S). Their handy work left an enormous sign proclaiming a word you shouldn't say in polite company.

## In Minnesota, Illic est Vinum

Most associate winemaking with California's sunny hills; however, Minnesota has its own proud winemaking tradition. The warmer, drier southern areas produce traditional wines from grapes, while the cooler northern latitudes get more creative, using local fruits such as raspberries, apples and strawberries. There is even a regional wine that combines fruit and honey. Now if that isn't a sweet deal, I don't know what is.

### Things That Go Bump in the Night
Minnesotans know how to keep warm on a cold night, and let's just say it doesn't always involve blankets. The state's residents boast a healthy sexual appetite that manifests itself in several ways...

## Good News for Recruiting

Trojan Condoms ranked the University of Minnesota as the number one university in the country for safe sex. The rubber-pushers chalked this up to emergency contraception, tests for sexually transmitted diseases, 10,000 free condoms and a condom-shaped mascot nicknamed Shady. When Dr. Ed Ehlinger, director of the university's Boynton Health Service Clinic, was told of the results, he replied, "This is the best news I've heard all day...We're number one in something—that's good." The study noted an impressive two-thirds of all students at the U of M were sexually active.

## Alternative Lifestyle

Minnesotans have long been accepting of the gay community.
In Minnesota, there are gay clubs, associations and leagues for
everything from books to choirs to hockey.

### It's Not Quite Amsterdam, But It Will Do…

All locals know of a kinky little spot in downtown Minneapolis
called Sex World. Whether you are looking for sexy lingerie,
toys requiring batteries or new copy of Sexopoly, Sex World is
the place to go. It is a good thing the store is open 24 hours a
day, seven days a week; its website lists over 15,000 movie titles.
For those adventurous souls (well, you probably wouldn't go
there if you didn't have an adventurous soul), there is something
called Kong Dong, which can only be described as a mechanical
bull for adults.

# Where To Be Seen

With a large population and numerous gay bars, Minneapolis is undoubtedly the headquarters of the Minnesota gay scene. At the epicenter of that culture are two popular hangouts.

The first, the ultra-popular Gay '90s Bar, offers a diverse entertainment lineup. Everything from drag shows to karaoke make the Gay '90s popular with both gay and straight patrons.

The other popular hangout is Loring Park. The Rainbow Families Conference in the spring and the GLBT (Gay, Lesbian, Bisexual and Transgendered) Pride Parade and Ashley Rukes Festival in June are two of the most prominent gay-themed yearly events in Minneapolis. The Pride Parade turns into a defacto "who's who" of the gay community. In addition to the parade featuring bedizened members of the gay community, vendors sell themed products and food, and GLBT-themed organizations try to make people familiar with their missions. "Rainbow" families attend the June festival, but so do singles and sympathetic straight neighbors.

DID YOU KNOW?

In 2007, Princeton Review rated Macalaster College in St. Paul "#1 best quality of life" and "#1 gay community accepted."

# FROM FARMS TO FACTORIES

Minnesota's first settlers came to take part in the state's robust fur trade and logging industry. As time moved on, and settlers with a background in farming moved to the area, the state's focus shifted to agriculture. However, no one would have predicted the explosion of the industrial, manufacturing and high-technology sectors on which Minnesota's economy now relies.

### Living the Good Life

Generally speaking, Minnesotans live a pretty good lifestyle. If the beautiful landscape wasn't enough, the state boasts the United States' eighth highest (second for states not on the coast) per capita income, with earnings of an impressive $37,737 per person. Areas around the Twin Cities have the highest per capita income, while the counties in Greater Minnesota lag behind. In addition, the state has a paltry unemployment rate of four percent.

In 2005, 71 percent of Minnesotans over the age of 16 were employed, the highest of any state in the nation. In addition to a stellar per capita income, Minnesota's cities feature a lower cost of living than cities of comparable size throughout the country. And those places can't touch Minnesota in the unquantifiable "enjoyment of life" factor.

## Damn Taxes!

With three brackets for state income tax (5.35 percent, 7.05 percent and 7.85 percent), Minnesota's tax structure is considered mildly progressive. Minnesota ranks as the sixth highest in the nation for per capita total state taxes. While the state sales tax is 6.5 percent, there is no sales tax on clothing (one of the reasons the Mall of America is in Minnesota!), prescription medications, limited service industries and groceries. With all those tax dollars, Minnesota is able to offer perhaps the best social services of any state in the nation.

DID YOU KNOW?

Minnesota's legislature really doesn't want you to smoke. The state features one of the highest tobacco taxes anywhere. Also, in the fall of 2007, smoking was banned in all restaurants and bars.

## Farming the Land

Minneapolis, the state's largest city, got its start as an agricultural hotbed. Merchants used St. Anthony Falls, the only waterfall on the Mississippi, to power the flour mills, which garnered Minneapolis the nickname "Mill City." Today, agriculture accounts for only one percent of the state's total economy, but it is a powerful force nonetheless. Minnesota ranks sixth nationally in the value of products sold and is the country's largest producer of sugar beets, sweet corn, green peas for processing and farm-raised turkeys.

# Is It Still Wild?

There is an old Native American adage that goes, "Do it the old way and it will stay." In Minnesota, farmers are only allowed to harvest wild rice the traditional way in order to safeguard the state's supply. They must harvest the crop by shaking it manually from the plants, usually into a canoe. The state's "wild" wild rice supply is all but gone; however, the crop is still grown commercially in Polk, Beltrami, Aitkin and Itasca counties.

### Going Yellow to Go Green

Minnesota opened a state-of-the-art ethanol plant in 1993 and has been rolling out barrels of the yellow stuff ever since. In 1997, Minnesota became the first state in the nation to mandate the use of ethanol, requiring all gas to have at least 10 percent—bumping up to 20 percent in 2013. In addition, more than 300 service stations supply the new E85 fuel. Although the "green" benefits of ethanol are debatable (in some regards, ethanol is actually worse for the environment), use of the fuel lessens the amount of foreign oil brought into the country and gives farmers a new market for their crops.

Minnesota boasts over 400 growers of Christmas trees in the state. These growers provide nearly 900,000 trees, valued at over $30 million. Those figures rank the state eighth nationally in Christmas tree business.

# Land O' Butter

Although often overshadowed by its neighbors to the east, Minnesota sports a robust dairy industry. Chief among those dealing in dairy is Land O' Lakes, a cooperative based in Arden Hills. With over 350,000 member farmers, Land O' Lakes is the largest food-marketing cooperative in the United States, grossing $6 billion in 2003.

# A Vegetable Giant

On a trip to England in the early 1900s, Ward Cosgrove of Minnesota Valley Canning Company (MVCC) brought back a pea unknown to North American farmers. Because of the pea's large size, Ward called the product "green giant." MVCC was later renamed Green Giant, after its signature product. To help market the peas, Green Giant developed a, well, green giant, and made him jolly. The Jolly Green Giant, along with his little friend, Sprout, has been the company's main marketing tool for over 75 years. Pillsbury (and in turn, General Mills) now owns the corporation, but the company's biggest advertisement can still be seen in Le Sueur. Today, Green Giant is the largest seller of frozen vegetables in the U.S.

MINNESOTA MAGIC

The first commercial to feature the Jolly Green Giant aired in 1953 but was deemed too frightening to young viewers and was pulled immediately. However, the Jolly Green Giant's jingle lives on:

*(Fo, fum, fo, fum)*
*Ho, hum, hi, he's*
*The Jolly Green Giant you see on the label*
*With golden corn and tender peas*
*The Jolly Green Giant will set up your table*
*With golden corn and tender peas*
*The Jolly Green Giant, 'tis he*
*The Jolly Green Giant, 'tis he.*

# HOMEGROWN HEADQUARTERS

*Maybe it is the clean air, maybe it is all the land to build lake homes, but whatever the reason, Minnesota houses an impressive number of corporations.*

## Bringing Khaki Back

When George Dayton founded Dayton's in 1902, he had no way of knowing what he started. Hundreds of stores, and billions of dollars later, Target Corporation is the fifth largest retailer in the United States and ranked number 33 on the Fortune 500 list. With Dayton's holding strong as an upscale department store, Dayton set out to create a discount retailer. He named his creation Target, to distance it from his prize baby, Dayton's. The Target story serves as an example of son eating father. In 2000, the company name was officially changed from Dayton Corporation to Target Corporation—with Target earning 75 percent of the Dayton Corporation's revenue. Today, the Dayton Corporation only lives on in the memories of Minnesotans—the stores were bought out by Marshall Fields, which was bought out by Macy's.

**DID YOU KNOW?**

The first Target was built in Roseville, a suburb of St. Paul. The company refers to the store as T-1, and the original building existed until 2005, when a new Super Target was built in its place.

## The Sound of Music

When Minnesotans hear "The Sound of Music" they don't think of Austrians singing in the hills; they think of electronics.

That's because one of the state's largest companies, Best Buy, started out as with the familiar title of The Sound of Music. That name held until a tornado hit the Roseville store and destroyed it. Later, when the store was rebuilt, stockholders made the bright decision to rename the company Best Buy, changing the logo to the familiar blue and yellow price tag.

DID YOU KNOW?

Best Buy is the largest private electronics dealer in the United States and Canada, accounting for 17 percent of the market. That's a whole lot of things to plug in!

## A Company for Champions

One of Minnesota's oldest companies is also one of its most profitable. Originally known as the Minnesota Milling Company, General Mills, at one point, operated one of the largest mills in the world. No longer a milling company per se, General Mills now offers an impressive array of food products. Together with its sister companies (some of which include Betty Crocker, Yoplait, Colombo, Totinos, Jenos, Pillsbury, Green Giant, Old El Paso and Cheerios), General Mills offers enough food diversity to tempt even the finickiest eaters. General Mills also specializes in marketing their products. Their Wheaties cereal boxes—and trademark "Breakfast of Champions" slogan—is a "who's who" in the sporting world.

DID YOU KNOW?

On average, consumers place at least one General Mills–affiliated product into their carts every time they go grocery shopping? Talk about filling the breadbasket!

# Keeping It Private

In addition to food companies, Minnesota hosts two of the largest private companies in the world. Cargill, Inc., founded in 1865, specializes in farm products and was responsible for 25 percent of all United States grain exports in 2006. The company has recently made the shift from producing and trading agricultural products to research and development of processing techniques.

The other private giant is Carlson Companies, located in Minneapolis. The company is a leader in the travel and hospitality industry, owning over 5400 travel agencies and 1700 hotels, resorts, restaurants and cruise ships worldwide. Now that is Minnesota hospitality at its finest!

Those aren't the only companies proud to call Minnesota home. Here are some other notables:

- Andersen Windows
- Aveda
- Caribou Coffee
- Cub Foods
- Ecolab Inc
- Geek Squad
- Imation Corporation

- Medtronic
- Northern Tool and Equipment
- Northwest Airlines
- Schwan Food Company
- SimonDelivers
- St. Jude Medical

- Supercuts
- Supervalu
- TCF Bank
- Toro
- U.S. Bancorp
- UnitedHealth Group
- Xcel Energy

Carlson Companies was voted one of the 100 Best Companies for Working Mothers.

# INTERESTING INNOVATIONS

*There is one benefit to Minnesota's spit-freezing winters—once the snow starts flying, Minnesotans have a lot of time to spend toiling in their workshops, finding the next great invention. From shoes that roll to paper that sticks (but not too much), you would be hard-pressed to find a state that has contributed more innovations that you use every day.*

## An Extra M

The name reads 3M (an abbreviation for Minnesota Mining and Manufacturing), but today it might as well be 2M—the company cut mining out of their business plan years ago when their biggest mining venture failed to turn a profit. So if mining no longer applies, maybe the extra "M" should stand for "mix up." That's because 3M owes much of it success to, well, mistakes.

The company began by mining a product that few people wanted, and even fewer knew how to use. A later switch to producing a waterproof sandpaper allowed the company to make a modest profit, but real success didn't present itself until 1925, when 3M invented what is now known as Scotch Tape. The tape, which could be removed easily from any surface without leaving a sticky residue, was a big hit in the auto industry.

Even the name of 3M's wundertape began with problems. In an effort to cut production costs, 3M scientists only put adhesive on the edges. One unsatisfied customer told the sales person to "Take this tape back to your Scotch bosses, and tell them to put some adhesive on it." Today, along with Scotch Tape, 3M produces various other products in the "Scotch" line, including Scotchgard and Scotchlite.

Scotty Mc-Tape, a kilt-wearing cartoon figure, was 3M's tape mascot in 1944, and continued to be so for two decades. The brand's familiar plaid logo, echoing a Scottish tartan, was created in 1945.

## Posting a Success

In 1974, an employee of 3M named Arthur Fry used a little divine inspiration to lift 3M to a whole new level. Being a good, church-going Lutheran, Fry wanted to sing in his church choir. The only problem was that the small paper bookmarks he placed in his hymnal continually fell out. That is when Fry remembered a presentation by one of his colleagues at 3M, Dr. Spencer Silverstein, who had talked about his wondrous new sticky papers. Silverstein had tried for nearly 10 years to get someone at 3M to care about his invention, but received a lukewarm reception. However, with Fry's backing, the duo took their idea to the powers-that-be at 3M. The product failed wondrously—or so they thought. As it turns out, the product only failed because consumers did not try it.

With a renewed effort, 3M did a free giveaway of the newly named Post-it Notes in Boise, Idaho. Over 90 percent of those polled said they would buy the product if it were available. It took 3M only three years to sell Post-it Notes nationwide. Today, 3M is one of the top five office suppliers nationwide. If that doesn't make you believe in a God, I don't know what else will...

## Cooling Your Car

If you were to guess where truck air conditioning began, you would probably guess a sultry climate such as Florida or Louisiana, right? Wrong. Truck air conditioning began in the heart of Minnesota. A chilly entrepreneur named Fred Jones thought of the invention in order to help a friend who owned a trucking business and continually lost food as a result of thawing. Jones and his friend started a company called Thermo King and, in addition to truck air conditioning, altered their design for airplanes, railroad cars and ships.

But Jones didn't stop at air conditioning. Throughout his life, the wild entrepreneur claimed over 50 patents, including portable x-ray machines, movie-ticket dispensers and motors for ice cream makers.

**You Put What in a Cannon?**
In 1901, Alexander Pierce Anderson blew the grain industry apart, literally. Anderson, a scientist from the river town of Red Wing, was working in New York when he had an idea that had never occurred to anyone over the course of human history. He thought it would be a good idea to put rice in a test tube, seal the tube airtight, and light it on fire. When he opened the heated canister, the rice popped like popcorn. Anderson immediately patented the idea and set about improving his invention. He finally arrived on a puffing cannon that used air to pressurize the rice and shoot it out. His invention debuted at the St. Louis World's Fair, where many people no doubt asked, What the hell good is that for? The answer, of course, is puffed rice cereal!

DID YOU KNOW?

The first automatic toaster "popped up" in Minneapolis in 1926. McGraw Electric Company named their creation the Toastmaster and sold it for $13.50.

## Making Winter More Accessible

Say what you like about the Minnesota winters, they inspire remarkable creativity. When you are penned inside your house for six months, you are likely to get bored. That is exactly what happened with three creative thinkers near the Canadian border town of Roseau. In 1954, Edgar and Allan Hetten and David

Johnson, bored with cross-country skiing (can you blame them?) looked for a more American way to cross wide expanses of snow. Their solution? Start a company called Polaris Industries and invent the snowmobile.

The group's first model was less than a success. Perhaps it was because they used a grain silo conveyor belt as a track and an old Chevy bumper for skis. Nevertheless, they sold their contraption to a man named "Silver Pete" (all business success stories should involve a man named "Silver Pete") and set about improving their design. The first mass-produced model debuted in 1956, weighed close to 1000 pounds and moved a rather unimpressive 20 miles per hour.

Today, however, Polaris is a bit more up to date on technology. They are the largest producers of snowmobiles worldwide and employ upwards of 1500 people—roughly one-tenth of the population of Roseau!

But the story doesn't end there. In 1960, after a fit of rage, Edgar left the group and started his own company in nearby Thief

River Falls and named it Arctic Enterprises (later Arctic Cat). The two companies remain intense competitors, inspiring fierce rivalry between the towns. Wearing a Polaris jacket in Thief River Falls is the equivalent of wearing a Yankees jersey in Fenway Park.

# Busy Busses

They say necessity is the mother of invention. That adage came true in the early 1900s in the small northern town of Hibbing. As result of the expansion of mining territory, the entire town had to be relocated. But how do you move a town? Well, if you are Carl E. Wickman and Andrew G. Anderson, you invent the bus!

The pair ordered a vehicle hefty enough to carry large groups of people. Their vehicle, probably the world's first bus, made the duo so much money that they were able to start or buy several other bus lines throughout the U.S. Perhaps you have heard of their company; today they go by the name Greyhound Corporation and provide affordable transportation to budget-minded travelers all over the country.

### For the Love of Hockey

In 1980, Minnesota youths Scott and Brennan Olson took an old idea and breathed new life into practicing hockey and staying in shape during the off-season. It seems they came upon a used, in-line skate in a secondhand store in Minneapolis. Using that idea as a prototype, the brothers transformed a hockey boot by replacing the blade with rollers and adding a rubber brake. The end result was a pair of rollerblades, and Rollerblade, Inc. was born. The Olsons ran their young company from the basement of their parents' home, but sold the company in 1984.

If it wasn't for forward-thinking Minnesotans, we wouldn't have these inventions either: bundt pans, HMOs, and Bisquick pancake mix.

# LIVING LONG

## Life Expectancy

Not only is there a lot to see and do in Minnesota, but you will also have a lot of time to see all the state has to offer. A 2006 study by Harvard ranked Minnesota as having the second highest life expectancy of any state. The only state ranked higher was Hawaii, while Mississippians have the quickest route to the undertaker. Minnesota men can expect to live on average 76.2 years, and Minnesota women can expect a robust 81.8 years. That is higher than 98 percent of the rest of the United States population!

Nicollet County in Minnesota boasts the 11th highest life expectancy of any county in the nation—an amazing 81.1 years. That is a whole lot of winters!

## "M" is for Muscle

Maybe it's the prevalence of dairy products and cholesterol-laden beef, or maybe it's the storing of fat for the cold winter, but whatever the reason, residents of Midwestern states tend to carry a few extra pounds. However, while other Midwestern states suffer from alarming obesity rates, Minnesotans are exceptionally fit. A 2005 study ranked Minnesota 36th out of the 50 states in obesity, finding that only 19 percent of the state's residents were "a bit on the pudgy side."

*Men's Fitness* magazine ranked Gustavus Adolphus College in St. Peter as the sixth most fit college in the nation. The magazine was exceptionally complimentary of the school's culture of fitness and the diverse fitness options offered.

## United in Health

The United Health Foundation, a nonprofit health agency, produces a report card each year of the nation's health and wellness. Each state is individually ranked in 18 different categories ranging from community environment to public health and policy. The report serves as an annual checkup and reminder to the state to note areas where growth is needed. As you might guess from the previous sections, Minnesota ranked exceptionally well. The state came in first in the nation for the fourth consecutive year, ranking among the top 10 states in 10 of the 18 measures. The report noted Minnesota's strengths as "a low rate of uninsured population at 8.4 percent, a low rate of deaths from cardiovascular disease at 239.8 deaths per 100,000 population, a low premature death rate with 5546 years of potential life lost before age 75 per 100,000 population, a low infant mortality rate at 5.1 deaths per 1000 live births and a low percentage of children in poverty at 10.0 percent of persons under age 18."

In addition, the report challenged Minnesota to improve its limited access to adequate prenatal care of pregnant women and moderately high violent crime rate.

Minnesota has the fewest deaths related to cardiovascular issues in the United States. Maybe winters so cold they can freeze your blood aren't so bad after all.

## Drowning in the Drink

For as healthy as Minnesotans are, one area of concern relates to alcohol-related issues. A 2005 study found Minnesotans had the third highest binge-drinking rate (19.8 percent) and 10th highest heavy drinking rate (5.5 percent) of any state in the nation. While no one doubts Minnesotans ability to party, these numbers are cause for some worry. On the brighter side, though, Minnesota finishes behind their neighbor to the east, Wisconsin, in both categories!

DID YOU KNOW?

Minnesotans practice safe sex! The state ranks 44th in the nation in chlamydia, with only a paltry 213.4 cases reported for every 100,000 residents.

*Minnesotans love the outdoors and do not hibernate in the winter. You have never lived until you have ice-fished on the middle of a frozen lake at night and you hear large cracking noises as the ice adjusts.*

–Mark, Le Sueur

# MARVELS OF MEDICINE

## Hold the Mayo!

Dr. William W. Mayo, a little-known English surgeon in pioneer-era Minnesota, began what would become the Mayo Clinic in 1883 (then known as St. Mary's Hospital). His sons eventually joined his practice, and the clinic quickly built a reputation as not only one of the finest hospitals in the area but also in the world.

While building a reputation for medical excellence, the Mayo family also built considerable wealth. Their family mansion, known as Mayowood, contained more than 38 rooms. One story relates that the house was so big that the younger Mayo boys kept pet goats in the basement for two weeks before their father even found out the goats were there. However, without a doubt, the house's most unique—err, scary—feature is the greenhouse. Constructed using thousands of glass x-ray plates, the interior reveals numerous misaligned body parts.

Today the Mayo Clinic is famous for treating world leaders, celebrities and common people—often as a last resort. The clinic continues the standards of excellence set forth by its founders 125 years ago.

**DID YOU KNOW?**

Dr. William W. Mayo pioneered the use of microscopes in diagnosing diseases.

### A Terrific Tandem
In 1915, the Mayo Clinic teamed up with the University of Minnesota to form the most formidable health-care team in the world. Since the merger, the duo continues to set the trend for cutting-edge research.

## Medical Milestones

The nation's first open heart surgery took place at the University of Minnesota in 1952. Surgeons Walton Lillehei and John Lewi operated on a five-year-old patient to repair a hole in the heart. As with any claim to fame, this one has been disputed. The African American Registry dates the first open heart surgery to 1893. It was believed to have been performed in Provident Hospital in Chicago by African American Dr. Daniel Hale Williams on a young man suffering from a stab wound.

# Other Medical Firsts

The University of Minnesota claims several other medical firsts in its stellar history, such as in 1968 when the first successful bone marrow transplant was performed on an infant. Here are a few more:

☛ First clinical use of cortisone therapy took place at the Mayo Clinic in 1950.

☛ The first heart-lung machine was developed in 1955.

☛ The first cardiac pacemaker was used in 1958.

☛ The University of Minnesota Hospital conducted the first pancreas transplant in 1966.

☛ The first implantable drug pump for diabetics was developed in 1975.

☛ On October 3, 1977, doctors at the University of Minnesota Hospital used the bi-leaflet mechanical heart valve for the first time.

☛ In 1979, artificial blood was used in a patient for the first time at the University of Minnesota Hospital.

☛ Stem cells were identified and isolated from adult bone marrow for the first time in December 2000. Professor Catherine Verfaillie and her research team were credited with the findings.

(Source: University of Minnesota)

# AN EDUCATED STATE

*Say what you like about Minnesota's weather, funny accents and perpetually losing sports teams, but you can't say anything bad about the state's 2743 public schools. From preschools to universities, Minnesota offers the best education of any state in the nation. Find that hard to believe? See if your opinion changes after reading this chapter.*

## High Scores for High Schools

Minnesota ranks consistently among the top states in preparing students for college. Although no one likes taking standardized tests, research connects scores on standardized tests, such as the ACT, with future college performance. In 2007, Minnesota students ranked first in the nation—for the third consecutive year—in composite ACT scores. The state average score was 22.5, almost a point and a half higher than the national average of 21.1.

Additionally, Minnesota ranked first in the nation in the percentage of residents with at least a high school diploma. With an 84 percent graduation rate, Minnesota ranks fifth in the nation in high school graduation.

**DID YOU KNOW?**

The top-ranked district in Minnesota for ACT scores was the Moundsview District, which includes Moundsview and Irondale high schools.

### Keeping the Mind and Body Activity

Minnesota schools pride themselves on the myriad extracurricular activities offered. Whether it is sports, clubs or service projects, Minnesota schools afford the opportunity for students to flex their creative and athletic muscles.

Although Minnesota has chosen not to implement school vouchers, the state was home to the first charter school.

# Higher Education

Colleges are everywhere in Minnesota—the only thing more common than an institution of higher learning are complaints about the weather. Minnesota features 34 private colleges and universities, 13 state colleges and universities (including five branches of the University of Minnesota) and 31 community and technical colleges. Add to the mix several medical colleges, law schools and seminaries, and you have a whole lot of learning going on.

**Golden Gophers**
Chief among Minnesota's numerous colleges and universities is
the University of Minnesota-Twin Cities. Located on the east
and west banks of the Mississippi River in the Twin Cities, the
school was the first chartered university in the state—and
remains the state's largest and best known.

# University of Minnesota-Twin Cities

Established: 1851

Location: Minneapolis and a small section in St. Paul

Nickname: Golden Gophers

School Colors: Maroon and gold

**Fast Facts**
- Locals refer to the school as "The U."

- With 50,402 students, the university claims the fourth highest number of students of any school in the country.

- The university has recently set an explicit goal to become one
  of the top three public research universities in the world
  within a decade. Although this seems ambitious, many of the
  school's programs are nationally ranked by the National
  Research Council: chemical engineering (1), healthcare
  administration (2), geography (3), teacher education (3), psy-
  chology (7), mechanical engineering (8) and economics (10).

- Signs reading "The Gopher Way" lead students to a series of
  underground pathways around campus for use on ultra-
  blustery days.

- "The U" may struggle to compete with other schools in the
  "big sports" of football and basketball, but the men's hockey
  team is one of the best in the nation. Herb Brooks (also from
  Minnesota) recruited nine players from the university to win
  the gold medal in the 1980 Olympics. In recent years, the
  women's team has established themselves as a national power.

## Notable Alumni
Sciences

- Ernest O. Lawrence, Nobel Prize in Physics

- Louis J. Ignarro, Nobel Prize in Physiology or Medicine

- Edward C. Prescott, Nobel Prize in Economic Sciences

- Dave Kapell, inventor of magnetic poetry

Arts

- Robert Penn Warren, Pulitzer Prize winner in 1947 for the novel *All the King's Men*; won the Pulitzer Prize in poetry in 1958 for *Promises: Poems 1954–1956* and in 1979 for *Now and Then*

- Carol Bly, author

- Bob Dylan, singer/songwriter (dropped out)

- Garrison Keillor, author

Sports

- Ric Flair, professional wrestler

- Bud Grant, former NFL coach

- Dave Winfield, Hall of Fame baseball player

Most of Minnesota's private colleges compete in a conference known as the Minnesota Intercollegiate Athletic Conference (MIAC). As a result of their long traditions (almost all the schools started in the 1800s) and close proximity, there are several spirited athletic rivalries. But the school features more than just athletic battles—the conference is a bastion for academic scholarship. Nearly every school in the conference receives mention in the U.S. News and World Report or the

Princeton Review's ranking of the top colleges in the country, including six in the top 100.

So next time you are in the area, check out a game or walk the campus at one of these stellar schools. With that many smart people, you are sure to hear some well-formed and creative debates.

## Augsburg College

Established: 1869

Location: Minneapolis

Nickname: Auggies

Colors: Maroon and gray

## Fast Facts

☛ The college houses the Minnesota Indian Teacher Training Program.

☛ Augsburg is a nationally recognized leader in providing services to students with physical or learning disabilities.

☛ The largest concentration of Somali immigrants in the United States is located next to the Augsburg campus.

## Notable Alumni

☛ Lute Olson, basketball coach at University of Arizona

☛ Martin Sabo (1959), former U.S. Representative

☛ Reverend Herbert W. Chilstrom (1954), first presiding bishop of the Evangelical Lutheran Church in America.

# Bethel University (formerly Bethel College)

Established: 1871

Location: Arden Hills

Nickname: Royals

Colors: Blue and gold

## Fast Facts

☛ Students and full-time faculty must abide by a Covenant for Life Together, a lifestyle agreement focusing on living a Christian life of personal morality, which includes a respect for all persons and ethnic traditions, refraining from extra-marital sex, gambling and the use of alcohol, illegal drugs and tobacco in any form.

☛ The school changed its name in 2004 to Bethel University to better reflect the broad academic programs offered.

☛ The school has satellite seminary campuses on both coasts.

**Notable Alumni**

☞ Joel Hodgson, creator of (and main character in) Mystery Science Theater 3000

☞ Ron Tschetter, director of the Peace Corps

# Carleton College

Established: 1866

Location: Northfield

Nickname: Knights or Carls

Colors: Maize and blue

**Fast Facts**

☞ The school's strong academic reputation draws students from not only all over the country, but all over the world as well.

☞ The nation's oldest student-run pub, the Cave, was founded at Carleton in 1927 and continues to host live music shows and other events several times each week.

☞ Peter Turk of The Monkees was a student of English at Carleton for three years until he dropped out to pursue music full time.

☞ A yearly campus softball game known as Rotblatt is a day-long event featuring copious drinking and a little bit of sport. The event drew praise from both *Sports Illustrated* and *ESPN: The Magazine*. This is the only time a Carlton sport drew praise.

☞ The popular computer game The Oregon Trail was created by students at Carleton in 1971.

☞ Each year Carleton plays crosstown rival St. Olaf in a foot-ball game dubbed the Cereal Bowl because of the proximity of Malt O' Meal, with the winner taking home the Goat Trophy. Carleton hasn't won the game in 13 years.

**Notable Alumni**

☞ Pierce Butler (1887), Supreme Court Justice (1923–39)

☞ Melvin R. Laird (1942), secretary of defense (1969–73)

☞ Barrie M. Osborne (1966), producer of the *Lord of the Rings* film trilogy

☞ Jonathan Capehart (1989), Pulitzer Prize–winning journalist

# Concordia College

Established: 1891

Location: Moorhead

Nickname: Cobbers

Colors: Maroon and yellow

**Fast Facts**

☞ The nickname "Cobbers" harkens back to Moorhead's rural heritage.

☞ First-year students are given bright yellow beanie hats during orientation and are supposed to wear them throughout their orientation week until the last day, when everyone gathers on Olin Hill and throws them up into the air.

☞ The college is located next to Prairie Home Cemetery, the inspiration for Garrison Keillor's Prairie Home Companion radio show.

☞ Superstition holds that students who walk through the bell tower alone will not get married, and Cobbers who walk as a pair will get married to each other.

**Notable Alumni**

☞ Coya Knutson, U.S. congresswoman (1955–59)

☞ Gary Larsen, NFL defensive tackle for the Minnesota Vikings

☞ Rich Sommer, actor, *The Devil Wears Prada*

# Gustavus Adolphus College

Location: St. Peter

Established: 1860

Nickname: Gusties

Colors: Black and gold

**Fast Facts**
- The school hosts the annual Noble Conference, featuring experts on scientific topics. Past conferences include "Prescription for Tomorrow" (2006) and "The Legacy of Einstein" (2005).

- In 1998, the school lived up to its "Gusties" nickname when a massive F3 tornado struck during spring break. The tornado caused $50 million in damage, but only killed one person (not a Gustavus student).

- Gustavus is the first private school in Minnesota to not require an ACT or SAT score for admission.

**Notable Alumni**
- Henry N. Benson, Minnesota attorney general (1929–33)

- Peter Krause, actor

- Luther Youngdahl, Minnesota governor (1947–51)

- Steve Zahn, actor

- Patsy O. Shermann, co-inventor of 3M Scotchgard

# Hamline University

Established: 1854

Location: St. Paul

Nickname: Pipers

Colors: Scarlet red and gray

**Fast Facts**

☛ Although the University of Minnesota was chartered three years earlier, in 1851, Hamline was the first university in Minnesota to admit students.

☛ The original campus was in Red Wing but moved to St. Paul in 1880.

☛ In 1869, the university shut down its operations after enrollment dropped drastically as a result of the Civil War.

☛ The university refers to itself as the birthplace of college basketball. Athletic director Ray Kaighn, who played with James Naismith, brought the sport to the campus in 1863. The school played the first college basketball game against what is now the St. Paul campus of the University of Minnesota. Hamline lost 9–3.

☛ The school takes its name from the Pied Piper of Hamelin, one of the Grimm Brothers' tales, in which a man plays his a pipe to first lure the rats out of town, then later does the same with the children when the town fails to pay him. Not a comforting thought for parents leaving their children there...

**Notable Alumni**

☛ Jim Gehrz (1979), Pulitzer Prize–nominated photographer

☛ Vern Mikkelsen, Hall of Fame basketball player

☛ Tony Reineccius, hockey player

# Macalaster College

Established: 1874

Location: St. Paul

Nickname: Scots

Colors: Blue and orange

## Fast Facts

☛ Alex Haley wrote part of the Pulitzer Prize–winning novel *Roots* in the apartment that now houses the International Center.

☛ The school is one of the most diverse in the Midwest: international students represent 90 different countries and comprise 14 percent of the student body; all 50 states and the District of Columbia are represented; and 20 percent of students are non-Caucasian.

☛ The "Grand Avenue Snowball Fight" takes place the evening of the first snowfall. Students from the north side of campus line the north side of Grand Avenue, and the students from the south side of campus take the south side of the street, and each side pelts the other with snowballs, much to the dismay of the St. Paul police.

## Notable Alumni

☛ Cass Gilbert, architect of the Minnesota State Capitol

☛ Kofi Annan, former secretary general of the United Nations

☛ Tim O'Brien, author of *The Things They Carried* and *In the Lake of the Woods*

☛ Walter Mondale, former vice president

# College of St. Benedict

Established: 1913

Location: St. Joseph

Nickname: Blazers

School Colors: Red and white

## Fast Facts

☛ It is one of only two all-female institutions in the MIAC.

☛ Affiliated with St. John's University, the students have different campuses but share an academic program.

**Notable Alumni**
☛ Laura Lundquist, noted school psychologist

# College of St. Catherine

Established: 1905

Location: St. Paul

Nickname: Wildcats or Katies

School Colors: Purple and black

**Fast Facts**
☛ One of two all-female institutions in the MIAC, St. Kate's is the largest all-female private college in the nation.

☛ The school boasts one of the top nursing programs in the nation.

☛ Former sister school of St. Thomas when St. Thomas was an all-male school.

☛ St. Catherine was the nation's first fully accredited Catholic women's college.

**Notable Alumni**
☛ Betty McCollum, current U.S. congresswoman

☛ Ruth Koscielak, local radio personality

☛ Emily Niemeyer Anderson, inventor of sour-cream-and-onion-flavored potato chips

☛ Pamela Wheelock, executive vice president and chief financial officer of the Minnesota Wild

# St. John's University

Established: 1857

Location: Collegeville

Nickname: Johnnies

School Colors: Cardinal and blue

**Fast Facts**

☛ St. John's claims the winningest football program of all time in NCAA D III history

☛ Head football coach John Gagliardi's record of 450-120-11 makes him the most successful college football coach in history—at any level.

☛ The campus offers Master's of Divinity and Master's of Arts degrees. The school also prepares seminarians for the priesthood.

☛ The school's rivalry with the University of St. Thomas culminates each year with a football game known as the Tommie-Johnnie game. Students at both schools create humorous T-shirts that mock the other school.

**Notable Alumni**

☛ Jon Hassler, novelist

☛ Eugene McCarthy, former U.S. senator

☛ Stephen Sommers, director for *The Mummy* and *The Mummy Returns*

# St. Olaf College

Established: 1874

Location: Northfield

Nickname: Oles

School Colors: Black and gold

## Fast Facts

☛ St. Olaf receives mention in F. Scott Fitzgerald's opus *The Great Gatsby*, in which the title character, Jay Gatsby, briefly attends the school but finds it "ferociously indifferent to his drums of destiny."

☛ The popular TV show *Golden Girls* pokes fun at the fictional city of St. Olaf—there is some debate as to whether or not this is a reference to the college.

☛ "Um Yah Yah," the school song, is the only polka college fight song in the country.

☛ The school's cafeteria was ranked second for the best college cafeteria in the country by the Princeton Review.

☛ St. Olaf's choir has preformed for numerous heads of state, including President George W. Bush and the King of Norway.

☛ With over 120 study abroad opportunities and 73 percent of students studying abroad, the school sends a higher percentage of students abroad than any other school in the United States.

## Notable Alumni

☛ Russell A. Anderson, chief justice of the Minnesota Supreme Court

☛ Robert Bly, poet

☛ Dean Buntrock, founder of Waste Management, Inc.

☛ Paul Henze, CIA Middle East Station Chief

☛ Ole Rolvaag, author, *Giants in the Earth*

☛ Sidney Rand, former president of St. Olaf, former U.S. ambassador to Norway

# University of St. Thomas

Established: 1885

Location: St. Paul

Nickname: Tommies

School Colors: Purple and gray

**Fast Facts**
- Legend holds that to become a true Tommie, one must kiss another Tommie under the arches at midnight.

- William Finn gave the land on which the school now sits to John Ireland, the school's founder. Finn received the land as compensation for shooting himself in the finger while on patrol in the Mexican-American War.

- The direct-to-video movie *Overnight Delivery* starring Reese Witherspoon was shot on the St. Thomas campus in 1998.

- William O'Shaughnessy, kicked out of the University of St. John's, enrolled at St. Thomas. Later in life, O'Shaughnessy struck oil and made millions. Upon his death, his estate bequeathed money to several places, including St. Thomas. The only stipulation was that no money could go to St. John's.

- Summit Avenue, which runs through the middle of campus, is the United States' largest stretch of Victorian-era houses.

**Notable Alumni**
- Will Steger, polar explorer

- Jim Oberstar, U.S. congressman

- Dottie Cannon, Miss Minnesota USA 2006

- Richard Schulze (Hon.), founder and CEO of Best Buy

# GET OUT AND VOTE!

*It is an understatement to say Minnesotans are politically active. Minnesotans vote, and vote often. In the 2004 presidential election, over 72 percent of eligible voters cast a vote at their local polling station—the highest percentage of any state and over 12 percent higher than the national average.*

## Let's Make a Deal

St. Paul was originally chosen to be the state's capital. However, Minneapolis (then known as St. Anthony) and Stillwater also laid claim to that honor. In a passive-aggressive decision that defined Minnesota interactions for years to come, the state decided to keep the capital in St. Paul, gave Minneapolis the university, and Stillwater received the prison.

DID YOU  KNOW?

In September 1901, Teddy Roosevelt's famous "Speak Softly, But Carry a Big Stick" speech debuted at the Minnesota State Fair.

 Minnesota is one of a handful of states that offers same-day voter registration. All a voter needs to do is go down to his or her polling station and fill out the required paperwork.

## A Political Party

The *major* political parties in the state are the Democratic-Farmer Labor Party (DFL), the Republican Party and the Independence Party of Minnesota (IP). The DFL formed in 1944 when the Minnesota Democratic Party and the Farmer-Labor Party merged.

Minnesota is traditionally considered a blue state, meaning the state carries a liberal perspective and left-leaning ideas. The state's left-wing stance went on the national stage in 1984 when Minnesota was the only state to vote for the Democratic, home-grown Walter Mondale, instead of Ronald Reagan. (Well, so did Washington, DC, but DC isn't a *real* state.) Minnesotans have sided with the Democratic candidate in every presidential election since 1976, the longest streak of any state.

DID YOU  KNOW?

Either Walter Mondale or Hubert H. Humphrey were on the Democratic ticket as candidates for president or vice president in the 1964, 1968, 1976, 1980 and 1984 elections.

# Taking a Swing

In recent years, Minnesota's liberal ways met a challenge from emerging right-wing conservatives. The state is now considered a swing state and has received considerable attention from campaigners in recent presidential races. Along with Wisconsin and Iowa, Minnesota forms an area politicians refer to as "the block" and carries as many electoral votes (27) as Florida. And we all know how well voting works in Florida...

Minnesota was one of the first states to ban discrimination in hiring and housing based on sexual orientation.

# Wrestlin' Up Votes

Although the state's largest "Third Party" is the Independence Party of Minnesota, it was the Reform Party's 1998 improbable gubernatorial victory that established independent party politics in Minnesota.

Running as a no-nonsense, common-man, Jesse "the Body" Ventura earned the right to be the first former pro-wrestler to run a state. Born in 1951 in suburban Minnesota, Jesse Janos was a member of the Navy Underwater Demolition Team. However, no one remembers "Jesse," as he is now known in the state, for his diving ability—they remember him for his feather boas, movie roles and leg drops. With little political experience (he was only the mayor of a small to medium suburb before his run), Jesse's candidacy caught some off guard. Pundits said he was a long shot against the political juggernauts, former St. Paul mayor—and current senator—Norm Coleman (Republican) and former Minnesota attorney general Hubert "Skip" Humphrey (Democratic Farmer Labor). Despite spending considerably less money (a paltry $600,000), Jesse's aggressive grassroots campaign and slogan, "Don't vote for politics as usual," garnered the former body slammer an unprecedented victory. The "Governor Body" led the state for four successful, if not outspoken, years before fulfilling his campaign promise of not running again.

While Ventura was governor, several wise entrepreneurs cashed in on the new governor's resumé. Most entertaining were the shirts, stating "Our governor can beat up your governor."

Despite his controversial comments in a *Playboy* (yes, *Playboy*) interview (in which Ventura said, "Organized religion is a sham and a crutch for weak-minded people who need strength in numbers. It tells people to go out and stick their noses in other people's business."), Ventura holds the record for highest approval rating of any Minnesota governor—an impressive 73 percent, or roughly 300 times higher than that of President George W. Bush.

## A Fantastic Defeat

Walter Mondale holds an honor no one would wish for. Running in 1984 against the popular incumbent, Ronald Reagan, Mondale suffered a severe beating. Mondale lost every state but one—his home state, Minnesota. Minnesotans are nothing if they are not loyal—and liberal!

Mondale's vice presidential candidate, Geraldine A. Ferraro of New York, was the first woman to run as the vice president on a major party ticket.

### Not Quite as Progressive as You Would Hope

In 1909, Minnesota's failure to pass a women's suffrage bill apparently led one understandably angered Minnesota woman to comment, "The women of Turkey will have the right to vote before we do in Minnesota!" Sadly, she was right, as Turkish women began voting in 1910. It would be another nine years before Minnesota's women would be allowed to enter the voting booth.

## A Governor with Flair

One of Minnesota's most enigmatic governors not to wear wrestling tights was Rudy Perpich. The son of Croatian immigrants, Perpich first took office in 1982. During his years in office, he set several benchmarks for a Minnesota governor. He was the first Roman Catholic governor, the longest-serving governor (eight years) and the first to win, lose, and then win again.

## The Original HHH

Before Triple H was body slamming wrestlers, Minnesota's own HHH was throwing politicians onto the canvas of the political arena. Credited with bringing the civil rights movement to Minnesota, Hubert H. Humphrey quickly rose up the political ladder. A *Star Tribune* columnist by the name of Kevin Duchschere boasted that Humphrey "would almost single-handedly transform Minneapolis' image from a corrupt backwater of crime and bigotry into a progressive city of clean and efficient government." In 1964, HHH was elected vice president by President Lyndon B. Johnson. However, HHH's presidential aspirations were quashed at the hands of Richard Nixon in 1978. And we all know how well that turned out…

# Lefty Liberal

One of Minnesota's most famous politicians is probably its most left leaning. Saying Paul Wellstone was liberal is like saying the ocean is wet. Born to Ukrainian Jewish parents in 1944, Wellstone quickly set about his goal to change the world. While working on his PhD at the University of North Carolina at Chapel Hill, he wrote a dissertation on "Black Militants in the Ghetto: Why They Believe in Violence." He then moved on to a professorship at the bastion of all things liberal, Carlton College in Northfield. However, Wellstone's antics proved too much for even the administration at Carlton—he was almost fired and needed a student sit-in (students are *always* holding sit-ins at Carlton) to save his job. In 1970, he became the youngest professor to ever earn tenure at the college.

Wellstone first was elected to office in 1990, defeating the highly favored Rudy Boschwitz in a close United States senate race. He then defeated Boschwitz again in 1996, when Boschwitz attacked Wellstone's liberal methodology—calling him Senator "Wellfare." Wellstone ran again for the United States senate in 2002, but died in a tragic accident just 11 days before the election.

Wellstone was known as a champion for the poor and disenfranchised. In addition to his work for those less fortunate, he was an eternal advocate for peace—he voted against both Desert Storm and the Iraq War in 2002, one of only 11 senators to vote against both. Although he sported one of the most partisan voting records of any senator, Wellstone's legacy is that of a man who worked tirelessly for what he believed.

DID YOU  KNOW?

Wellstone was known for campaigning in a distinctive green bus. His unique mode of transportation is the subject of a documentary entitled *The Magic Green Bus.*

# The First Lady

In a state of firsts, Minnesota also boasts the country's first female ambassador. Eugenie Anderson lived a rather quiet life in southern Minnesota until she began to get politically active as World War II swept across the country. Her post-war campaigning for Harry Truman and Hubert H. Humphrey led to her position as United States ambassador to Denmark. Two years later, Anderson made another historic first when she became the first American woman to sign a treaty. She ended her career as United States ambassador to Bulgaria.

# Political Prominence

Here's a sampling of other prominent politicians who called Minnesota home:

☞ Frank B. Kellog, secretary of state under Calvin Coolidge, 1925

☞ William Windom, secretary of treasury under James Garfield, 1881, and Benjamin Harrison, 1889

☞ Alexander Ramsey, secretary of war under Rutherford B. Hayes, 1879

☞ William D. Mitchell, attorney general under Calvin Coolidge, 1929

☞ Orville L. Freeman, secretary of agriculture under John F. Kennedy and Lyndon B. Johnson, 1961

☞ Bob Bergland, secretary of agriculture under Jimmy Carter, 1977

☞ Maurice H. Stans, secretary of commerce under Richard Nixon, 1969

☞ James Day Hodgson, secretary of labor under Richard Nixon, 1979

# FINE ARTS

## Great Guthrie

In 1959, Sir Tyrone Guthrie placed a small ad looking for nothing more than a city interested in creating a community theater. Of the seven cities that replied, the Twin Cities seemed the most eager to partake in Guthrie's plan. Guthrie desired a new kind of theater that would encourage the production of great works and cultivate actors' talents away from the more commercial environment of Broadway.

The Guthrie Theater first opened its doors on May 7, 1963, with a production of Hamlet, with George Grizzard playing the lead, directed by Tyrone Guthrie himself. Over the course of its illustrious history, the Guthrie Theater grew from a small play-house to a big player on the national dramatic stage. Today, the Guthrie Theater is the largest regional playhouse in the country.

One of the theater's most popular productions is the yearly rendition of Charles Dickens' *A Christmas Carol*.

The Guthrie Theater moved to a new, three-theater complex after its closing 2006 production, Hamlet, on May 7, 2006.

DID YOU KNOW?

Minneapolis is home to the oldest continuously running theater (Old Log Theater) and the largest dinner theater (Chanhassen Dinner Theater) in the country.

# MIA

No, not missing in action; in Minnesota, the acronym MIA stands for Minneapolis Institute of Arts. Started by the Minnesota Society of Fine Arts, the MIA first opened its doors in 1915. Designed by the preeminent New York architectural firm McKim, Mead and White, the neoclassical building expanded in 1974 with an addition designed by the late Japanese architect Kenzo Tange. In June 2006, the museum unveiled a new wing designed by architect Michael Graves. Housing more than 100,000 pieces of the world's finest art, the MIA serves as one of the largest art galleries in the Midwest. Each year more than half a million people visit the collection.

# LITERATURE LEGACY

## Speaking for an Era

From his birth on Cathedral Hill in St. Paul, it was clear F. Scott Fitzgerald was destined for big things—he weighed a knee-quaking 10 pounds, 6 ounces. Always an outsider, Fitzgerald strove for belonging and social acceptance among St. Paul's wealthy class. Later in his life, Fitzgerald wrote, "The rich are different from you and me."

Fitzgerald attended the prestigious St. Paul Academy, where he met more resistance. So displeased were his fellow pupils that they took out an ad in the school newspaper looking for a person willing to "poison Scotty or find some means to shut his mouth."

Fitzgerald left Minnesota in 1922 and never looked back. Speaking about Minnesota, he said, "I no longer consider Minnesota my home...I never could quite adjust myself to those damn Minnesota winters...though many events there will always fill me with a tremendous nostalgia." Fitzgerald's Minnesota heritage appears several times in his later writing. Here are some notable instances:

- Nick Carraway, Fitzgerald's loveable protagonist in *The Great Gatsby,* hails from Minnesota.

- The novel's title character, Jay Gatsby, talks about his time in Duluth and attending St. Olaf College.

- His short story "The Ice Palace" centers around St. Paul's curious obsession with its annual building of an ice castle.

Fitzgerald may have distanced himself from Minnesota, but he is still known as St. Paul's first successful novelist. Today, Fitzgerald's legacy remains in nearly every high school English course and in the term the "Jazz Age," which Fitzgerald coined to describe the affluence and social meanderings of his time.

**DID YOU KNOW?**

F. Scott Fitzgerald's full name is Francis Scott Key Fitzgerald, and he is named after one of his star-spangled singing relatives.

**The Main Man**

While Fitzgerald is known for his retelling of life in high society, another Minnesota author made his career retelling small-town life. Born in rural Sauk Center, Sinclair Lewis left home at the tender age of 13. As most boys do, he harbored hopes of serving as a drummer boy in the Spanish-American War. With those dreams deflated, Lewis set about on the still-worthy path of becoming a Yale student.

Lewis' best-known work is the novel *Main Street*. From humble beginnings—publishers were only hoping to sell 25,000 copies—the book's down-to-earth pathos and satirical portrayal of small-town life became an instant success, selling two million copies. Lewis' biographer, Mark Schorer, stated the phenomenal success of *Main Street* "was the most sensational event in 20th-century American publishing history."

Sinclair Lewis' *Main Street* won the Noble Prize for Literature—the first American novel to claim the prestigious honor.

**DID YOU KNOW?**

*Main Street* centers around life in Gopher Prairie, a pseudonym for Lewis' hometown of Sauk Center—and it is also an homage to Minnesota's loveable vermin.

## Writing for Peanuts

St. Paul native Charles Schulz brought a whole new meaning to "writing for peanuts." His comic strip first appeared in the *Star Tribune* but soon went into national syndication. Today, it's hard to imagine a time when Charlie Brown and his loveable friends didn't exist. St. Paul honors Schulz's comic strip each year by featuring statues of different characters throughout the city. Local businesses purchase the statues and decorate the artwork as they wish.

# A Little Book That Made It Big

While she isn't from Minnesota (she hails from the land time forgot to the east), Laura Ingalls Wilder does the state proud. Writing about her time growing up in the late 1800s, Wilder captured the hearts of adults and little children alike. Her earnest and heartwarming prose details her time in Walnut Grove and events such as surviving the grasshopper plague of the 1870s. Her Little House books inspired a 1970s TV series that made cloth frocks and rag dolls seem cool.

And yes, Virginia—and every other youngster who's ever been engrossed in Laura's stories—there is a Walnut Grove. In fact, the same sod hut where the Ingalls family first lived in 1874 has been unaltered all these years, even after they left their Minnesota farm in 1876. The 172-acre farm was purchased in 1947 by Herman and Della Gordon, and once they were made aware of its historical significance, the family continued to maintain the dugout and welcome visitors. Just 1.5 miles away, in Walnut Grove, the Laura Ingalls Wilder Museum chronicles the history of the real family, along with their fictional television counterparts. As well, the community hosts a pageant every summer, during which a Laura-Nellie Look-Alike Contest is held.

# Telling It Like It Is

Garrison Keillor (born Gary Keillor, he changed his name to "Garrison" to sound more poetic) had a penchant for story telling that began during his childhood in the Plymouth Brethren community. That's what happens when TV, radios and movies are shunned.

Keillor rose to fame by creating the beloved radio show *A Prairie Home Companion*. The first installment was broadcast over the airwaves of Minnesota Public Radio (MPR) on July 6, 1974. The show took a brief sojourn in 1986, before starting up again shortly afterwards. While most broadcasts emanate from the Fitzgerald Theater in St. Paul, Keillor often takes the show on the road.

The show is a haven for folk music, and the most popular bit remains Keillor's "News from Lake Wobegon"—"Where all the women are strong, all the men are good-looking, and all the children are above average." But don't search for Lake Wobegon on any map, because, according to legend, it was left off the maps because of the "incompetence of surveyors who mapped out the state in the 19th century." The town may be fictional, but for many, Keillor's musings harken back to a simpler time and remind listeners of their youth. A look at the town's businesses and other staples recall a time when things moved a bit slower:

☞ Ralph's Pretty Good Grocery: "If you can't find it at Ralph's, you can probably get along without it."

☞ The Sidetrack Tap, run by Wally and Evelyn: "The dim little place in the dark where the pinball machine never tilts, the clock is a half-hour slow, and where love never dies."

☞ Chatterbox Café: "The place to go that's just like home."

☞ Art's Bait & Night O'Rest Motel

☞ Our Lady of Perpetual Responsibility Catholic Church, with Father Emile

☞ Lake Wobegon Lutheran Church, with Pastor Ingqvist

☞ Bunsen Motors, the local Ford dealership run by Clint and Clarence Bunsen, local Lutherans

☞ Krebsbach Chevrolet, run by Donnie Krebsbach, local Catholic

☞ The *Harold* (*Herald*) *Star*, town newspaper run by Harold Star

☞ Skoeglins Five and Dime

☞ LuAnn Magadance's Bon Marchaise Beauty Parlor and Salon

☛ The Sons of Knute

☛ The Whippets, the town baseball team

☛ The Herdsmen, the champion ushering team

Keillor parlayed the success of *A Prairie Home Companion* into several successful books, all of which feature life in the quiet town. Acclaim for the show also produced a 2006 movie largely based on the radio program. The movie failed to achieve success at the box office because of both the casting of Lindsay Lohan and the complete absence of references to Lake Wobegon. That just shows what the listeners really want!

Popular writer Tim O'Brien was born in Austin, Minnesota, and attended Macalaster College in St. Paul. O'Brien's two favorite topics to write about are the Vietnam War and Minnesota.

# FILMED IN MINNESOTA

## Lights, Camera, Action

Minnesota isn't exactly Hollywood (and to be honest, the residents wouldn't want it to be), but the state has produced its fair share of movies, commercials and television programs. The first and quite obvious reason Minnesota is chosen is because it provides a beautiful backdrop. Whether filming small-town farm life, untouched wilderness or a bustling city, Minnesota has it all.

The second and less boastful reason involves the numerous incentives the state provides to filmmakers. A program known as Snowbate offers production crews 15 percent back on all in-state expenditures related to making films, commercials, music videos or television programs. Additionally, expenditures for TV commercial production and post-production are exempt from Minnesota sales tax, and those who stay in the state for more than 30 days do not pay the state's lodging tax. The incentives are meant to entice filmmakers to the state, who will then spend their money to boost the economy. Also, filming in Minnesota shows off how great the state is!

And the program must be working because approximately 435 movies and television programs have been filmed in Minnesota. Here is a list of the top 50 movies filmed in the North Country:

1. Airport (1970)

2. Angus (1995)

3. Beautiful Girls (1996)

4. The Big One (1997)

5. The Cure (1995)

6. D2: The Mighty Ducks (1994)

7. D3: The Mighty Ducks (1996)

8. Drop Dead Fred (1991)

9. Drop Dead Gorgeous (1999)

10. Embrace of the Vampire (1995)

11. Factotum (2005)

12. Fargo (1996)

13. Feeling Minnesota (1996)

14. Friday the 13th: The Final Chapter (1984)

15. The Good Son (1993)

16. Grumpier Old Men (1995)

17. Grumpy Old Men (1993)

18. The Heartbreak Kid (1972)

19. Here on Earth (2000)

20. Highway 61 (1991)

21. Ice Castles (1978)

22. Iron Will (1994)

23. Jingle All the Way (1996)

24. Joe Somebody (2001)

25. Little Big League (1994)

26. A Little Trip to Heaven (2005)

27. Major League: Back to the Minors (1998)

28. Mallrats (1995)

29. Martha, Meet Frank, Daniel and Laurence (1998)

30. Michael Moore Hates America (2004)

31. The Mighty Ducks (1992)

32. No Direction Home: Bob Dylan (2005)

33. North Country (2005)

34. Overnight Delivery (1998)

35. A Prairie Home Companion (2006)

36. Purple Rain (1984)

37. Pushing Tin (1999)

38. Rollerball (2002)

39. A Simple Plan (1998)

40. Slaughterhouse-Five (1972)

41. Sugar & Spice (2001)

42. Sweet Land (2005)

43. Trauma (1993)

44. Trekkies (1997)

45. Twenty Bucks (1993)

46. Untamed Heart (1993)

47. Utvandrarna (1971)

48. Wisdom (1986)

49. With Honors (1994)

50. Youngblood (1986)

# TUNED IN TO TV

## She Made It, After All!

One of the best-loved TV shows of all time, *The Mary Tyler Moore Show*, took place in Minnesota. It depicted the life of Mary Richards (Mary Tyler Moore), who worked at the fictional TV station, WJM-TV. The show lasted for seven years and made stars of both Mary Tyler Moore and Minneapolis. A statue of Moore, in her trademark pose from the show's intro, remains poised on Nicolett Mall.

## Hey, Coach!

The school was fictional, but the success was real. ABC's TV series *Coach* detailed the events of a down-on-their-luck band of football coaches at the fictional Minnesota State. The show remained a success for several years, only failing when the producers moved the program to Miami, when the coach took an NFL job. Guess that shows what the fans really wanted to see!

# LEADING MEN AND LADIES

*All those movies filmed in Minnesota need actors and actresses to star in them—so it should come as no surprise that Minnesota has produced more than its fair share of Hollywood's leading stars.*

## There's No Place Like Home

Her birth certificate says Frances Ethel Gumm—but you know her better as Judy Garland (and isn't it better that way?). Born in Grand Rapids, Garland got her big break at her father's theater, where she danced with her sisters in the all-too-unfortunately named "Glum Sisters Trio."

Garland's career transformed when her family moved to California and she landed the role of Dorothy in the film version of *The Wizard of Oz*. Her role as the loveable, if not geographically apt, girl from Kansas scored her a special Oscar (children weren't awarded Oscars until much later) and an even more laudable singing career. One reviewer, speaking to the power of Garland's voice, notes that Garland possessed "a voice, that without P.A. system could be heard throughout the entire Chinese Theatre."

Fans of *The Wizard of Oz* and all things Judy Garland should consider a summer drive out to Grand Rapids for a tour of the Judy Garland Museum. Housed in the home where she lived the first four or so years of her life, the museum has an assortment of memorabilia commemorating her life in the world of entertainment and welcomes visitors to taste life as the young Judy experienced it. She died on June 22, 1969, at the age of 47, and her talent was celebrated in a big way when Minnesota proclaimed June 22, 2006, Judy Garland Day. The city also hosts the Judy Garland Festival each June.

DID YOU KNOW?

Garland beat out everyone's favorite redhead, Shirley Temple, for the role of Dorothy. Do you think the ruby red slippers would have clashed with that red hair?

## A Real Ice Melter

Jessica Biel was born in Ely on the Canadian border; however, her family moved shortly after her birth. But who cares—she is the hottest thing to come out of the North Country since, well, ever. She may have moved some 20 years ago, but locals still credit her with melting the winter ice. How many states can say they spawned the "sexiest female" in 2007, according to *Maxim* magazine. Just one: Minnesota.

# The Male Heartthrob

Biel may have made her Minnesota exodus early, but the state's male heartthrob, Josh Hartnett, stuck around a bit longer. Growing up in St. Paul, Hartnett briefly attended prestigious Cretin Derham Hall before transferring to Minneapolis South. He first started to make the hearts of teenage girls beat a littler faster in the slasher flick, *Halloween H20: 20 Years Later.* His role of avoiding masked killers led to more noteworthy roles in *Blackhawk Down* and *Pearl Harbor.* Not one to cut his Minnesota roots, Hartnett often frequents the Twin Cities' trendy nightspots.

## Naming Rights

Winona Ryder is not only from Minnesota, but she is also named after one of its cities. In an extraordinary lack of creativity, her parents named her after the city where she was born (maybe they ran out of names after already choosing Yuri, Jubal and Sunyata for their other children). However, Winona didn't stay long in Minnesota—probably because of the lack of Saks 5th Avenue from which to steal.

 Gale Sondergaard of Litchfield was the first to win an Oscar for a supporting role. The actress of Scandinavian heritage won for her 1937 role in *Anthony Adverse.*

# The Best of the Rest

Some were born and got the hell out (their loss), while others maintain homes in the area. Regardless, the following actors and actresses all list Minnesota on their birth certificates:

| | | |
|---|---|---|
| Eddie Albert | Peter Graves | Sean William Scott |
| Loni Anderson | Jessica Lange | Kevin Sorbo |
| Rachel Leigh Cook | Michael O'Leary | Vince Vaughn |
| Ed Flanders | Nate Richert | Steve Zahn |

# MAKING MUSIC

*Minnesota boasts a vibrant and diverse music scene. Like many things, the epicenter of the state's music scene rests in the Twin Cities. However, areas of Greater Minnesota produce a strong folk music community.*

## Putting Minnesota on the Map

When you mention Minnesota to anyone not from the state, two things immediately come to mind. The first, the weather, was discussed at length earlier in this book. The second involves a small, high-pitched creature clad in purple—Prince, of course.

Born in 1958 just outside Minneapolis, Prince Rogers Nelson (yes, his name is actually Prince) came out of the womb the same height he is now. Prince showed an early inclination for eccentricity and music—both in large doses. He recorded his first album in 1978, playing all the instruments himself and wearing enough makeup to bedizen the entire cast of *America's Next Top Model*. Over the next 30 years, Prince went on to make both hits and headlines in equal numbers. With undeniable talent and a penchant for putting on a spectacle, Prince is one of the most enigmatic artists of our generation. While songs such as "When Doves Cry" and "Purple Rain" are timeless classics, Prince is best known for two things: the color purple (he once lived in a giant purple mansion in Chanhassen) and controversy (just do an online search for "Prince" and "controversy," and the results are sure to be hilarious).

Authors' note: At the time of writing, his name was still, in fact, Prince. For those of you reading this book later (perhaps only a year later), if he has changed his name to a color, symbol or sign for the zodiac, we apologize.

DID YOU  KNOW?

Los Angeles indie rock band, Sabrosa Purr, named their debut EP "Music From the Violet Room" after a misinterpreted Prince lyric in "The Ballad of Dorothy Parker" from *Sign o' the Times*.

## Getting Funky

Disco made a lot of people do things they regret. One of those things was the song "Funkytown" by the Minneapolis-based group, Lipps, Inc. (say it out loud to get the name). Now used for torturing confessions, the song was actually a number one hit at one point. While the song hints at the group's boredom with the Twin Cities, Minnesotans can rejoice in the fact that no one would willfully listen to the song anymore.

# All It Takes Is a Change of Names

There must be something in the water that makes Minnesota's musicians change their names. Everyone knows about the multi-monikered Prince, but do you know Robert Allen Zimmerman? Maybe you know him by his stage name, Bob Dylan—he chose the name for the Welsh poet, Dylan Thomas. Born and raised in northern Minnesota, Dylan briefly attended the University of Minnesota before traveling the country as a vagabond performer. These journeys inspired the anti-war song, "Blowin' in the Wind." With a stiff, unrefined voice, Dylan continued to produce hit after hit throughout the '60s and '70s. His protest and anti-war songs struck a chord (pun intended) with his generation, and he quickly grew to be one of America's top artists. In addition to countless other awards over his 40-plus year career, Dylan's "Like a Rolling Stone" was named the most influential rock song ever by *Rolling Stone* magazine—OK, maybe they were a bit biased.

DID YOU  KNOW?

Bob Dylan's career did not stop with the protests of the Vietnam War. Dylan found plenty to sing about in his 2006 release, *Modern Times*. The album topped the charts, making Dylan the oldest living person ever to hold that honor. It was later named album of the year by *Rolling Stone*—no bias, this time.

## Not All Can Be Winners

OK, so Minnesota produced some bands that, in retrospect, were never really that great. In 1986, the Jets really took off (and we can only wish they'd stayed away). Composed of the eight oldest siblings of a family of Tongan immigrants, the Jets topped the charts (with flattops, nonetheless) with such regrettable songs as "Crush on You" and "You Got It All."

Before the Minneapolis airport was stopping politicians from lewd acts (see the "Crimes and Criminals" chapter), they were holding down airplanes—Jefferson Airplane, to be exact. In 1970, officials caught one of the band's musicians, Marty Balin, hosting a rockstar-esque party at an airport hotel. That wasn't the problem. The problem was the possession of marijuana—and the presence of several underage girls. Balin never served any jail time, but he did have to continue wearing those ridiculous outfits.

## It's a Rap

You would think a state known for its Scandinavian heritage wouldn't be a hotspot for hip-hop—but you'd be wrong. In recent years, several of Minnesota's hip-hop acts have emerged from the oblivion of the north and taken the main stage. Led by the ultra-talented Atmosphere, and followed by Rhymesayers labelmates Brother Ali and Musab, Minneapolis hip-hop reached a new level of respect in the 21st century. Look out L.A. and New York—there's some new players on the block—and they're cold.

## The Best Place to See a Show

Wondering what to do on any given night? You can't go wrong catching a show at First Avenue (plus, it is easy to find, because the name tells you the location!). While larger arenas such as the Target Center and the Xcel Energy Center have their merits, you can't match the ambiance and unbridled energy of a show at First Avenue (simply known as "First Ave" to the locals). Formerly known as The Depot (the building used to be a Greyhound station), First Ave served as the springboard for almost every major Minnesota musician, including The Replacements, Prince, Soul Asylum, Semisonic, Atmosphere and Dillinger Four. An eclectic mix of performers playing the lovingly defiled venue means that no matter your music of choice, First Ave is sure to feature a show for you.

Other noteworthy venues featuring music sure to please your ears include The Fine Line Music Café, Bunkers and Harvey's.

First Ave was shut down in late autumn of 2004 for financial reasons, causing panic to strike in music fans in the Midwest. The issues were resolved quickly, but there was such a commotion that the judge presiding in the bankruptcy case noted, "I gather there is some urgency about this." Minneapolis mayor, R.T. Rybak, promised to do a stage dive at the first show after the club's reopening, but he thought better of the idea after learning the first show would feature the heavy metal band GWAR.

*My first impression of Minneapolis, Minnesota, was that it reminded me a little of Chicago without the traffic, litter and crime. Minnesotans are still exposed to great theater, cuisine and culture, but on a smaller scale. Lastly, it's a great place to raise children. I have a one-year-old daughter, and I couldn't think of a better place to raise her.*

–Alan, Chicago, Illinois

# WACKY LAWS

## Book 'Em

Lawmakers are supposed to have your best interests in mind when drafting laws—and for the most part, they do. However, one has to ask—what were the powers-that-be thinking when writing these laws? Each of the following laws appears either as state or local law. Is it sadder these laws exist or that somewhere, at sometime, these laws needed to be passed in the first place?

### State Statute 18.051: Declaration of Policy

*the abatement or suppression of mosquitoes of any kind, whether disease bearing or merely pestiferous, within any or all areas of the state, is advisable and necessary for the maintenance and betterment of the health, welfare and prosperity of the people thereof.*

Anyone who has spent a July night in Minnesota can understand this law, but does it really need to be public policy? Prosperity? Really?

### Cottage Grove Statute 7-3-3: Activities Requiring Permit

*No person shall engage in the following activities, except pursuant to a permit for the activity:*
*Section G: Use park property for starting or landing of aircraft, hot air balloons, parachutes or hang gliders.*

Well, at least you can use that new picnic table for landing your private jet in a pinch—just make sure you have the proper permit.

### Minnetonka Statute 845.010.11: Public Nuisances Affecting Peace, Safety and General Welfare

*The following are declared to be nuisances affecting public peace, safety and general welfare: a truck or other vehicle whose wheels or tires deposit mud, dirt, sticky substances, litter or other material on any street or highway.*

I guess this means you need to walk in Minnetonka when it rains? Wouldn't want to deposit mud on the road.

## Hibbing

*It shall be the duty of any policeman or any other officer to enforce the provisions of this Section, and if any cat is found running at large, or which is found in any street, alley or public place, it shall be the duty of any policeman or other officer of the city to kill such cat.*

Police officers must use this as practice for the hunting season.

# More Loony Laws

Here is further evidence that alcohol is served freely and openly when laws are written:

☛ Citizens may not cross state lines with ducks on their heads. If a person is crossing to Wisconsin, a chicken atop the head is also illegal.

☛ In Blue Earth, no child under the age of 12 may talk over the telephone unless monitored by a parent.

☛ A Minnesota tax form is quite thorough. Some would say too thorough. It even asks for your date of death.

☛ It's illegal to tease skunks. (As if being sprayed wasn't enough of a deterrent.)

☛ A woman isn't allowed to cut her own hair without her husband's permission.

☛ It is illegal to sleep naked.

☛ It used to be legal in Minnesota to sell rolled candy on Sunday, and illegal to sell flat candy. The wafer people have gotten this one repealed.

☛ In Clawson, it is legal for a farmer to sleep with his pigs, cows, horses, goats and chickens. Farm dogs must be OK.

☛ All Minnesota bathtubs must have feet.

☛ It is legal for a robber to file a lawsuit if he or she got hurt in your house.

☛ In Brainerd, every man is required by law to grow a beard.

☛ Hamburgers may not be eaten on Sundays in St. Cloud.

☛ In Harper Woods, it is illegal to paint sparrows to sell them as parakeets.

☛ In Duluth, it is illegal to allow animals to sleep in a bakery.

☛ Red cars are not permitted to drive down Lake Street in Minneapolis.

☛ Oral sex, while at one time prohibited, is now legal.

☛ In Alexandria, no man is allowed to make love to his wife with the smell of garlic, onions or sardines on his breath. If his wife so requests, law mandates that he must brush his teeth.

☛ In Rochester, all bathing suits must be inspected by the head of police.

☛ Smoking while in bed is illegal.

☛ There is a 10 cent bounty for each rat's head brought into a town office.

☛ You are not allowed to park your elephant on Main Street in Virginia.

## Jesse James' Justice

In September 1876, Jesse James and his Younger Boys gang rode into Northfield—but only a couple of them rode out. When the gang arrived in town, they found Main Street crowded for a convention, and the gang set their sights on the First National Bank of Northfield. While members of the gang spread themselves around town, three of the outlaws entered the bank. They immediately shot the cashier, Joseph Lee Heywood, and set about plundering the place. What the gang didn't know was that another storeowner sounded the alarm, went to his hardware store and handed guns to anyone who wanted them. When the bandits emerged from the bank, the townspeople were ready. Bob Younger was wounded, Clel Miller killed and William Stilles left behind in the ensuing gunfight. The others took off with quite a following—some estimates say 1000 townspeople chased after the gang for three weeks. The mob caught up to the gang near Madelia. The Younger brothers were taken to jail, while Charles Pitts refused to surrender and was killed. The only two who made it out with their lives were the James boys, who used stolen horses and the cover of night to ride to Missouri. The prize for their efforts? $290.

Each year in September, Northfield hosts Jesse James Days, featuring a reenactment of the famous gunfight. The Northfield
Historical Society Museum is housed in the bank the James-
Younger gang tried to rob. Along with information on Jesse
James and his band of outlaws, visitors can learn about the area's
history, along with that of the entire state. And rumor has it
that if you ask really nicely, you might get a tour of the basement
and see what some believe is a skeleton of one of the outlaws.

DID YOU  KNOW?

The famous capture of Jesse James might never have happened
had the gang not changed their plans. Originally the gang
planned to rob a bank in nearby Mankato; however, they found
the banks of Northfield too tempting a target to pass up.

If you are looking for a bank to rob, you might want to skip the First National Bank of Northfield. No one tried to rob the bank after the Jesse James incident—until 1994. Another attempt, same result—customers chased that guy down as well.

### Holding the Company "Ransome"

The Hormel Company almost went bankrupt in the 1920s. The company was doing splendidly until they hired Ransome J. Thomson to serve as the company's assistant controller. With money he claimed was inherited from a deceased relative, Thomson built a farm on the Minnesota-Iowa border. Oddly enough, Hormel's accounts were bleeding money. The founder's son, Jay Hormel, put two and two together and began to research the company's accounts. He found his new assistant controller had stolen over $1 million (yes, $1 million in Depression-era money) to pay for improvements to his farm. Thomson stole so much money that Hormel was unable to pay his creditors, and the company was almost foreclosed upon. Jay Hormel only saved the company by pledging everything he owned to guarantee the loans—and firing Thomson.

## Unhelpful Helper

A luckless thief pleaded guilty to the attempted robbery of a convenience store in Detroit Lakes. The thief told a passerby he was going to rob the store, gave the man a dollar and asked him to go inside and buy a scarf to hide his identity during the crime. The bystander took the dollar, went inside the store… and called the police.

## Save the Costumes for Halloween

After pulling off a successful armored car heist and pocketing a cool $34,000, a group of desperados decided to enrich themselves again, at the expense of Garda United Armor Services. This time, since their key member, Garda driver Nichole

Nelson, was still under investigation for the first heist, the group decided to make their move at the TCF Bank in Robbinsdale. Also, the new plan included roughing up Nelson to divert suspicion from her. Once on her route, Nelson sent a text message to her cohorts, giving them her schedule and alerting them to the number of guards inside the truck. The fatal flaw in the plan involved taping up their getaway rides with duct tape (not at all obvious!), then donning masks and face paint while sitting in the TCF Bank's parking lot. As expected, they were spotted and busted before they got to make their move on the armored truck.

*The two things that I love most about Minnesota are the trees and the water. When I go back home, I miss them and always look forward to seeing them when I'm returning. The undeveloped areas (lakes, swamps, ponds, etc.) in an urban area make it seem less artificial and more comfortable. As I drive around the Twin Cities, it's such a treat to see natural areas.*

–Laurie, Sioux Falls, South Dakota

# COMICAL CASES

*Truth is stranger than fiction, but it is because fiction is obliged to stick to possibilities; truth isn't.*
–Mark Twain

## Caution: Bullets Make Lions Unhappy

In 2003, Rolf Rohwer, a wildlife biologist from Scotland, filed a federal lawsuit against bullet manufacturers Federal Cartridge Co., of Anoka, Minnesota, and Trophy Bonded Bullets, Inc., of Houston, Texas. While Rohwer was on an African big-game hunting safari, he used a new type of ammunition, which he claims failed to stop a charging lion that attacked and injured

him severely. The bullet—a .458 Winchester Magnum, 500-grain Trophy Bonded Bear Claw—was advertised for use in big-game hunting. Louis Franecke, Rohwer's lawyer in San Rafael, California, alleges the ammunition was ineffective on the lion, stating, "This bullet is not suitable for killing a charging lion." The bullet, which is designed to expand on impact and kill big-game animals such as rhinoceros and hippopotami, passed through the thin skin of the lion. But rather than stopping the charging lion, the shot enraged the animal, which then mauled Rohwer. Officials with Federal Cartridge had no comment on the suit. According to his website, Rohwer has since returned to big-game hunting.

### Keeping It in the Family
A Minnesota man sued his parents in 2004 for employment discrimination after he lost his job at the family business. Steven Sarenpa alleges he was forced from his job because of an extra-marital affair. Sarenpa claims his parents were upset with his decision to leave his wife, and they chastised him at work, yelling at him and telling him there was no reason for adultery. Sarenpa filed a lawsuit in federal district court alleging that his parents discriminated against him based on their religious and marital beliefs. He claimed his parents, devout Christians, tried to force their religious views upon him at work. When he refused to end his relationship with another woman, Sarenpa claimed his parents created a hostile work environment. Sarenpa's parents denied any wrongdoing.

## Do Your Research

The Minnesota legislature passed a law that revoked state approval for any type of malt liquor that "states or implies in a false or misleading manner a connection with an actual living or dead American Indian leader." This law stemmed from the sale of Crazy Horse malt liquor, named after Tasunke Witko, leader of the Lakota Nation. Crazy Horse is famous for warning the Lakota against alcohol and its associated effects.

## How to Pass the Time

A convicted sex offender filed suit against state officials to prevent them from confiscating his video game console. Officials at the state hospital in St. Peter apparently mistakenly approved Arthur Dale Senty-Haugen's purchase of the video game console in June 2002, but after recognizing that the machine violated policy, they allegedly informed the convict he had to get rid of the console himself or have it confiscated and destroyed. Senty-Haugen filed his complaint in the Ramsey County District Court and claims that he relied on the video game console "for numerous daily activities including engaging in socialization and entertainment." According to Senty-Haugen's complaint, hospital officials believe the console is prohibited because it could allow him to connect to the Internet to download pornography, but the sex offender contends his activities are already carefully monitored. He also claims that he spent more than $1000 on the machine and video games. After losing previous administrative appeals, Senty-Haugen sought a temporary restraining order to keep on playing.

## You Put Your Right Hand In…

On June 11, 2007, a strange event occurred at the Minneapolis airport. An undercover police officer arrested Idaho senator Larry Craig for suspicion of lewd conduct. The arresting officer reported that Senator Craig trolled through an airport bathroom, frequently peeking through stall doors. Craig then entered the stall to the officer's left, and that is when things got really weird. The officer's report states Craig "tapped his right foot. I recognized this as a signal used by persons wishing to engage in lewd conduct. Craig tapped his toes several times and moved his foot closer to my foot…. The presence of others did not seem to deter Craig as he moved his right foot so that it touched the side of my left foot, which was within my stall area. Craig then proceeded to swipe his left hand under the stall divider several times, with the palm of his hand facing upward."

In speaking with the police officer, Craig claimed he simply had a "wide stance" (guess that term isn't just used for sports anymore) and that he was "simply trying to pick up a piece of paper." Whatever the result of the case, this will make you think twice before using a public bathroom. As if you needed another reason.

DID YOU  KNOW?

After news broke of Senator Craig's conduct, visitors to the airport began snapping pictures of themselves in front of the much-publicized privy.

## Twinkiegate

When Minneapolis city council candidate George Belair served Twinkies and other refreshments to two senior citizens' groups in 1985, he was indicted for bribery in what the newspapers dubbed "Twinkiegate." Although the charges were eventually dropped, the case led to a Minnesota fair campaign act, popularly known as the "Twinkie law." The law was repealed in 1988.

# THOSE PAID TO PLAY

*Being a fan of professional sports in Minnesota requires patience, understanding and, some would argue, a love of having your heart broken, over and over again. If the teams aren't in danger of contraction or moving (North Stars moved to Dallas; Lakers moved to Los Angeles), they fail to win championships. Apart from the Minnesota Twins' two World Series championships, the state's professional teams are "0-for-ever." Still, year after year, Minnesota sports fans pack the stands or crowd their TV sets to cheer on their beloved teams. Here are some snapshots of the state's most popular professional teams.*

## The Professionals

**Team:** Minnesota Vikings

**League:** National Football League (NFL)

**Division:** National Football Conference, North Division

**Year Founded:** 1961

**Venue:** Hubert H. Humphrey Metrodome (Minneapolis)

**Championships:** Not one

**Colors:** Purple, gold and white

**Mascot:** Viktor the Viking; Ragnar

**Interesting Facts**

☛ The Vikings were the first NFL team to play in, and lose, four Super Bowls.

☛ Joseph Juranitch, who plays the current mascot Ragnar, holds the world record for the shortest time shaving a beard with an ax.

☛ The Vikings went 46 years before introducing significant changes to their original uniforms.

☛ The Vikings fearsome defensive line of the '70s earned the moniker the "Purple People Eaters."

☛ Several Vikings players received national attention in 2005 for their partying on a local lake. The scandal, dubbed "Loveboat" by the local press, involved players allegedly paying for "dancers" and partying well into the night. That may not sound so bad, but the players did it on a family cruise ship, staffed by workers who, let's just say, weren't ready for the things they saw.

**Team:** Minnesota Twins

**League:** Major League Baseball (MLB)

**Division:** American League, Central Division

**Year Founded:** 1961

**Venue:** Hubert H. Humphrey Metrodome (Minneapolis); new stadium planned for 2008

**Championships:** Two (1987 and 1991 World Series)

**Colors:** Dark blue, red and white

**Mascot:** TC Bear

**Interesting Facts**

☞ The team was founded in Washington, DC, in 1901 and named the Washington Senators. The president moved and renamed the team the Minnesota Twins (for the Twin Cities) in 1961, awarding Washington, DC, with another team.

☞ The Minnesota Twins was the first professional baseball team named after a state instead of a city.

☞ In June 2006, the Twins became the first MLB team to boast the Player of the Month, Pitcher of the Month and Rookie of the Month.

☞ The Twins have notorious hazing rituals for their rookie relief pitchers—such as having the new pitcher carry snacks to the bullpen in a pink children's backpack.

DID YOU  KNOW?

When Fidel Castro was young, he tried out for the Washington Senators (now the Minnesota Twins). Castro showed some promise as a left-handed pitcher but couldn't throw a curve ball over the plate with any consistency. The team cut him before he could play a regular season game. The rest, as they say, is history. Although he never played for the Twins, Castro did pitch two innings in a 1960 post-season exhibition game between the Havana Sugar Kings and the Minneapolis Millers.

**Team:** Minnesota Timberwolves

**League:** National Basketball Association (NBA)

**Division:** Western Conference, Northwest Division

**Year Founded:** 1989

**Venue:** Target Center (Minneapolis)

**Championships:** Nope

**Colors:** Black, forest green, blue and silver

**Mascot:** Crunch

**Interesting Facts**

☛ The team name comes from a "Name the Team Contest" in Minnesota.

☛ In 1984, Governor Rudy Perpich assembled a 30-man team in an attempt to seduce the Milwaukee Bucks, San Antonio Spurs and Utah Jazz into moving their franchises to the state. Minnesota was eventually awarded a franchise five years later.

☛ The Timberwolves' dance team has over 50 outfits and never uses a routine more than three times.

DID YOU  KNOW?

Before Minnesota had the Timberwolves, they had the Minneapolis Lakers. (You didn't think they were actually named after lakes in L.A., did you?)

**Team:** Minnesota Lynx

**League:** Women's National Basketball Association (WNBA)

**Conference:** Western Conference

**Year Founded:** 1999

**Venue:** Target Center (Minneapolis)

**Championships:** Not yet

**Colors:** Blue, green, white and silver

**Mascot:** Prowl

**Interesting Facts**

☛ The Lynx was added as an expansion team to counter the addition of the Orlando Miracle.

☛ Since 1999, the Lynx have had two Rookies of the Year: Betty Lennox and Seimone Augustus.

☛ In 2004, point guard Teresa Edwards was the oldest WNBA player ever, at 40 years old.

**Team:** Minnesota Wild

**League:** National Hockey League (NHL)

**Division:** Western Conference, Northwest Division

**Year Founded:** 2000

**Venue:** Xcel Energy Center (St. Paul)

**Championships:** Working on that

**Colors:** Forest green, red, gold and white

**Mascot:** None

**Interesting Facts**

☛ The top six potential names for the team were the Minnesota Blue Ox, Minnesota Freeze, Minnesota Northern Lights, Minnesota Voyageurs, Minnesota White Bears and Minnesota Wild.

☛ Chief Financial Officer Martha Larson was the first female to hold that position in the NHL.

☞ In 1999, the Wild announced a 26-year partnership with the Minnesota Amateur Sports Commission—the first-ever professional/amateur pairing.

☞ The Wild do not choose a permanent captain; instead, the team rotates the honor each month.

**Team:** Minnesota Thunder

**League:** United Soccer League

**Division:** First Division

**Year Founded:** 1990

**Venue:** James Griffin Stadium (St. Paul)

**Championships:** One (1999 "A" League Championship)

**Colors:** Blue and gold

**Mascot:** Thor

**Interesting Facts**

☞ Although the team was founded in 1990, it did not become professional until 2004.

☞ The team's badge logo, when placed on a jersey, contains a gold star to commemorate the 1999 championship team.

☞ The team created an amateur women's team in 2006, named the Minnesota Lightening.

DID YOU  KNOW?

Minnesotan baseball commentator Halsey Hal was the first to say "Holy cow!" during a baseball broadcast.

# FOR THE LOVE OF THE GAME

*Although the professional teams are loveable in their losses, Minnesota also produces numerous amateur athletes and teams that could show their professional counterparts a thing or two.*

## Golden Gopher Hockey

The nickname may lack some tenacity (who the heck is afraid of a gopher, especially a golden one?), but the team's reputation is enough to strike fear in the heart of any opponent. While the rest of the state's teams struggle to win, the Golden Gophers from the University of Minnesota have six national championship banners, 12 Western Collegiate Hockey Association (WCHA) regular season championship banners and 14 WCHA playoff championship banners hanging from their arena's rafters. What makes these honors more impressive is the players. Almost all the players on the team are born and bred in Minnesota. Other schools may seek out (older) Canadian-born mercenaries, but the Golden Gophers win with skaters who honed their skills on Minnesota's frozen rinks.

Colorado may house many of the United States Olympic training facilities, but Minnesota has curling! The United States Olympic team trains at the Bemidji Curling Club. Curling can best be described as a sport that involves one person pushing a heavy rock down the ice, while teammates sweep the ice like a maid before a house party.

# A Saintly Appearance

Minnesota baseball fans who want to watch an outdoor baseball game should skip Minneapolis and head over to St. Paul to catch a Saints game. Although two previous minor league baseball teams in St. Paul also took the Saints name, the current team began in 1993 and plays in the Independent League. The Saints may offer a lower quality of baseball than their professional peers, but they win fans over with outdoor baseball and an environment where having fun trumps the actual game. The Saints feature a pig instead of a ball boy, a nun who gives massages and a hot tub in left field. Another reason fans back the stands (Saints tickets can be among the toughest in town to get) are the humorous and off-color promotions. Here are some favorites:

☛ During the 2002 MLB labor negotiations, the Saints gave away seat cushions with pictures of Commissioner Bud Selig on one side and player's association Executive Director Donald Fehr on the other.

☛ That same year, in response to Selig's controversial decision to end the MLB All-Star Game in a 7–7 tie, the Saints gave out ties with Selig's image.

☛ In August 2003, the Saints held "Randy Moss Hood Ornament Night," poking fun at the Viking's wide receiver, who was involved in an incident in which he bumped a traffic control officer with his car while attempting to make a turn.

☛ In 2006, the Saints gave away rubber boats, under the ruse they were to honor the 30th anniversary of the television show *The Love Boat*. However, the boats were same color as the Vikings uniforms (purple and yellow), and details indicate that the promotion was actually a jab at the 2005 boat scandal involving the Minnesota Vikings. In addition, the rubber boats were named *Minnetonka Queen* (a reference to Lake Minnetonka, where the cruise took place).

☛ In August 2007, the Saints gave out rubber dog toys to fans, as a dig at the federal dog-fighting case involving quarterback Michael Vick.

DID YOU KNOW?

The first cheerleader in the country was said to be Johnny Campbell. The University of Minnesota student apparently leapt onto the field during a football game on November 2, 1898, and led the crowd in a cheer.

## Minnesota High School Hockey Tournament

In late March, Minnesota school children get a welcome reprieve. No, it isn't spring break—it is the State High School Hockey Tournament. The event is so important that many schools allow students to have the day off to watch or attend the tournament. Held at the Xcel Energy Center, the event is the most watched and attended state tournament of any sport, in any state. Teams from all over Minnesota compete in two classes, divided by enrollment. From Warroad in the northwest to Winona in the southeast, the tourney consumes the fantasies of most boys and girls in the state. Instead of growing up hoping to hoist the Stanley Cup, young Minnesota hockey players dream of skating on the big rink. The event fosters heated rivalries and produces more local legends than you can count. Say the names Willard Ikola, John Mayasich, Neal Broten and Dave Spehar to any Minnesotan, and you will hear remarkable stories about goals scored and games won.

# THE VENUES

## Metrodome

First and foremost on the Minnesota sports scene is the much-maligned Metrodome. Rising over the city of Minneapolis like a bowl of sugar cubes, the Metrodome isn't what you would call aesthetically pleasing. Opened in 1982 and coming in $2 million under budget, the "Dome," as locals know it, remains the least-appreciated aspect of Minnesota sports—and for good reason. The Dome may be good for hosting a variety of events—everything from Vikings and Gopher football, Twins baseball and, at one point, Timberwolves basketball—but it doesn't do any of the sports justice. The Dome is especially brutal for baseball games. The viewing angles are as pleasant as a kick to the groin, and having a roof over your head while watching baseball is like wearing a blindfold to the movies. It isn't any better for the players, who complain that the white roof makes it impossible to see the ball. Who would have thought it would be a bad idea to use a white roof on a baseball stadium?

All quirks aside, the Dome has achieved a cult standing with both athletes and fans alike. But those days are coming to an end. In 2009, the Golden Gophers will open a new, on-campus football stadium, and the Minnesota Twins change addresses in 2010.

The Metrodome is the only facility in the country to host the World Series, a Super Bowl and a NCAA Final Four Basketball Championship game.

DID YOU  KNOW?

Major League Baseball umpires ruled Dave Kingman's 195-foot, vertically hit baseball a ground rule double when the ball entered—and stayed in—one of the 11-inch holes in the roof of the Metrodome.

## An Xceling Arena

When the NHL rewarded the city of St. Paul with another franchise, it was clear the city needed to build a venue worthy of the gift. The arena went beyond anyone's imagination. Named "one of the top five arenas in North America" by *ESPN The Magazine*, the Xcel Energy Center sets the standard for excellence and opulence in sporting venues. The "X," as locals refer to it, features wide concourses, numerous restaurants and many, many hockey-crazed fans. The arena set its attendance record of 19,484 during the 2004 NHL All-Star game.

 The Xcel Energy Center will host the 2008 Republican Convention.

DID YOU  KNOW?

When the home of the Timberwolves, the Target Center, opened in 1990, it featured more bathrooms than any other sports arena in the nation.

# NOTABLE SPORTS FIGURES

## Just Two City Kids

Minnesota has produced a laundry list of baseball talent, but two of its brightest stars were born in the same neighborhood, only four years apart. Dave Winfield and Paul Molitor grew up a few miles from each other, playing in St. Paul parks and recreation leagues.

Winfield, the older of the pair, went on to start at the University of Minnesota in both baseball and basketball. In baseball, he led the Golden Gophers to the College World Series as a pitcher. His career on the court was no less impressive, with his coach Bill Musselman calling him the finest rebounder he ever coached.

Winfield's athletic success paid off on draft day, four of them, actually. He was drafted by the San Diego Padres in the MLB, the Minnesota Vikings (despite not playing college football), the Atlanta Hawks of the NBA and the Utah Stars of the ABA. To this day, Winfield is one of only two men ever drafted in three different pro sports (the other being Dave Logan), and the only man to be drafted by four leagues. It gets even better. In 1974, playing off Winfield's proclivity for being drafted, the World Hockey Association gave Winfield's rights to the Minnesota Fighting Saints. Winfield chose baseball, and over his Hall of Fame career, he amassed 3000 hits and was, at one time, the highest paid player in baseball.

DID YOU  KNOW?

Winfield was traded to the Cleveland Indians at the trade deadline on July 31, 1994, for a "player to be named later." As all baseball fans remember, the 1994 season was cancelled two weeks later, so Winfield did not play for the Indians, and no player was ever named in exchange. To settle the trade, Cleveland and Minnesota executives went to dinner, with the Indians picking up the tab. This makes Winfield the only player in major league history to be traded for a dinner.

The other kid in town, Paul Molitor, went on to have quite a baseball career of his own. Despite a rough start that included numerous injuries (he once dislocated a knuckle when he stuck his hand in a teammate's glove) and a substance abuse problem, "Molly" earned the respect of fans and teammates alike. Over his stellar career, he won a World Series in Toronto, is one of only four players in major league history with at least 3000 hits, was a first-ballot Hall of Famer, had a .300 lifetime batting average and stole 500 bases.

There must be something in the water in that part of town. After producing Winfield and Molitor, that same neighborhood gave birth to baseball superstar Joe Mauer.

## From Tackles to Trials

Alan Page, a member of the vaunted Vikings Purple People Eaters, had a stellar football career. However, all the accolades in football can't match his later-life accomplishment. Playing football wasn't enough for Page; he had to go to law school while playing pro football full time. Go ahead, picture an NFL player doing that today! Upon retirement, Page went into private practice and eventually earned the role of assistant attorney general. But he wasn't done yet—Alan Page is now Justice Page, serving as a three-time Supreme Court Judge in the Minnesota Supreme Court.

## A Godsend for Gamers

Fans of video games would have missed a lot if it weren't for one Minnesotan. The king of all football games, John Madden, first stepped onto the gridiron in Austin. Everyone knows Madden for his video games and quirky commentator quips during games, but many would be surprised to know he was once a player in the NFL, spending a brief amount of time with the Philadelphia Eagles. Madden rose to prominence as a coach with the Oakland Raiders in the '70s. He led the Raiders to a Super Bowl win in 1970—however, he beat the hometown Vikings in that game.

# A Miracle Career

In 1980, Herb Brooks and his teammates gave the U.S. something to believe in during the Cold War by defeating the only unbeatable team in hockey. Born in 1937, Brooks won a state tournament with St. Paul's Johnson High School team in 1955, which earned him a scholarship from the University of Minnesota. Brooks was the last man cut from the 1960 U.S. Olympic hockey team, which won the gold medal, and it was something that has always stayed with him. He later played on the 1964 and 1968 Olympic teams. However, Brooks remains known for his miracle in 1980, when he coached the U.S. team to a win over the Russian juggernaut—and eventually secure a gold medal. Dubbed the "Miracle on Ice," many consider that win to be the single greatest upset in sports history. All Brooks did was lead a group of ragtag college kids to a win against the older, professional Russian players—who hadn't lost in 12 years. Brooks went on to coach and scout for several NHL teams before he died in a tragic car crash in 2003. His legacy met national attention with the 2003 Disney release of *Miracle*, which detailed Brooks' fiery and often obtuse coaching strategy.

DID YOU KNOW?

Mike Modano, whose career started with the North Stars in 1988, is the leading American-born scorer in NHL history.

# Kirrrbbby!

Minnesota's most enigmatic athlete isn't actually a Minnesotan at all—and even though Kirby Puckett wasn't born here, Minnesotans embraced him as if he were family. Born in the Robert Taylor Homes housing project in Chicago, Puckett's career had an inauspicious beginning. So unheralded was Puckett out of high school that he worked briefly at a Ford plant before joining a big league club. Although his career started

small, Puckett soon grew to legend status in Minnesota. His play championed the Minnesota Twins to both their World Series wins in 1987 and 1991 (when he made what is simply referred to as "the Catch"). Over his career he did nothing less than rewrite the record book for a Twins player.

Sadly, Puckett's later years were marred by scandal. He had to retire all too young when glaucoma ravaged his eyes. From there, things only got worse, with several lawsuits against the man who, though sporting a short stature, stood taller than Paul Bunyan. But Minnesotans are forgiving, and when Puckett passed away in 2006, fans wept openly as they made the pilgrimage to Puckett's de facto shrine at the Metrodome.

What made Puckett so popular was not his play—although that was in itself stellar—it was his "common man" demeanor. Despite all the accolades, ask any Minnesotan what he or she remembers Puckett for, and chances are you will hear about the joy with which he patrolled center field. No matter the outcome of a game, you could count on seeing Puckett out there with a boyish grin, patrolling center field with the innocence of a child. Boys and girls (and probably more than a few adults) scaled fences in their backyards trying to emulate "Pucks" and his oh-my-god-he-didn't-just-do-that plays. But no one ever could. No one could ever be Kirby.

In the end, Kirby's essence can be summed up by a quote he gave during his retirement ceremony, "Kirby Puckett's going to be all right. Don't worry about me. I'll show up, and I'll have a smile on my face. The only thing I won't have is this uniform on. But you guys can have the memories of what I did when I did have it on.

# TRIVIA TIDBITS

## This and That

Minnesota has too much of interest to pack into the previous sections of this book. Here are other things worth knowing about the great state of Minnesota:

☛ Because of soft limestone, the Falls of St. Anthony have moved approximately four miles upstream since their discovery.

☛ The St. Paul Chamber Orchestra (once called the St. Paul Philharmonic) was the first full-time professional chamber orchestra established in the nation.

☛ Joseph Rolette hid the bill that would have made St. Peter the capital of the state. He hid it in his hotel room until the constitutional time limit expired, thus keeping St. Paul the capital.

☛ Minnesota was the first state to offer troops to Abraham Lincoln to fight in the Civil War.

☛ The white sandstone found in southeastern Minnesota is composed almost entirely of quartz.

☛ Congressman Andrew Volsead of Granite Falls sponsored the Prohibition Amendment.

☛ The phrase "A common bond for all the arts" can be found on the seal of the University of Minnesota.

☛ In 1882, Minneapolis was home to the world's highest light fixture.

☛ Minnesota's waters flow in three directions: north to Canada's Hudson Bay, south to the Gulf of Mexico and east to the Atlantic Ocean.

☛ The University of Minnesota was one of the first in the nation to include condoms in the snack vending machines.

☛ The Minnesota Vikings have scored a total of 34 points in their four appearances in the NFL's Super Bowl.

☛ Eighty-three-year-old millionaire Elisabeth Congdon was murdered with a pink satin pillow by her son-in-law in 1977 in Duluth.

☛ Native Minnesotan Richard Sears perfected the home catalog industry—and formed the Sears & Roebuck Company.

☛ Famous architect Frank Lloyd Wright once designed a gas station in Cloquet.

☛ In the First Battle of Bull Run in the Civil War, the First Minnesota Regiment had more losses than any other northern regiment.

☛ The state's first three-term governor was John S. Pillsbury.

☛ The Minnesota Historical Society was established in 1849, nine years before Minnesota officially became a state.

☛ *Travels Through the Interior Parts of North America*, which details Jonathon Carver's expedition through Minnesota, has been through 53 known editions in nine countries since its first publication in 1778.

☛ The University of Minnesota is home to the world's first university School of Nursing, which began in 1909.

☛ Prior to his national political years, Eugene McCarthy taught sociology at the College of St. Thomas.

☛ Minnesota's birthrate in 1980 was the same as it was in 1933.

☛ According to Minnesota mythology, a snowstorm always occurs during the state high school basketball tournament.

☛ The Northwest Angle of Minnesota is not connected to the state by land.

☛ The Minnesota company Honeywell helped perfect World War II airplane controls and proximity bombs.

☛ The Redjackets, a former NFL franchise, began in Minneapolis in 1929.

☛ Hematite causes some of the rocks and soils in the state to assume a reddish color.

☛ Five percent of the state's area is water.

☛ Minnesota's state flower, the lady's slipper, will die if a flower is plucked from the plant; however, left untouched, the lady's slipper has a 100-year lifespan.

☛ Minnesota has the most nesting northern bald eagles in the contiguous states.

☛ There are 11 miles of paved streets on the state fairgrounds.

☛ St. Olaf College beat archrival Carleton College 43–0 in the nation's first metric football game, held in 1977.

☛ On September 28, 1969, Minnesota Viking Joe Kapp threw seven touchdown passes while playing Baltimore.

☛ There were approximately 31.5 million acres of virgin forest when the first white settlers arrived in Minnesota.

☛ Minnesota's 1920s-era exclusive Naniboujou Lodge had such guests as Babe Ruth and Jack Dempsey.

☛ Minneapolis firefighter Lewis Rober invented the game of kittenball, which was later called softball.

☛ Seymour Cray, a University of Minnesota alumnus, built the first supercomputer.

☛ Alexander Ramsey was the first leader of the Republican Party in Minnesota.

☛ The nation's first Better Business Bureau was founded in Minneapolis in 1912.

☛ Bloomington and Minneapolis are the two farthest north latitude cities to host a World Series game.

☛ The rocks in the Boundary Waters Canoe Area are over three billion years old.

☛ In 1919, a Minneapolis factory turned out the nation's first armored cars.

☛ Hudson Bay is the closest body of salt water to Minnesota.

☛ Ralph W. Samuelson invented water skis in 1922, when he bent eight-foot-long pine boards into skis.

☛ Hastings took its name from Minnesota's first governor, Henry Hastings Sibley.

☛ In 1979, a patient at the University of Minnesota received the first artificial blood transfusion. He was a Jehovah's Witness and said that a real blood transfusion conflicted with his religious beliefs.

☛ From where it starts in Lake Itasca to the Gulf of Mexico, the Mississippi River stretches slightly over 2500 miles.

☛ Minnesota was once covered by the prehistoric Lake Agassiz.

☛ The United States Government offered the Sioux people 12 cents per acre, to be paid over a 50-year span, in the Treaty of Travers de Sioux.

☛ The Minnesota Legislature was the first in the nation to ratify the Amendment to the United States Constitution lowering the voting age to 18.

☛ There is nearly twice the number of single men than single women in rural Minnesota.

☛ Minnesota has provided more Olympic and professional hockey players than any other state.

☛ Minnesotan Ann Bancroft was the first woman to reach the North Pole on foot.

☛ Worthington was settled in 1871 by the National Colony Company, which prohibited the sale of liquor.

☛ Midway Stadium was originally built with the intention of luring the Brooklyn Dodgers to Minnesota.

☛ One of Minnesota's longest school bus routes is along 120 miles of the Gunflint Trail.

☛ Local brew Hamms Beer has the slogan "From the Land of Sky Blue Waters."

☛ Minnesota's Interstate 35 can be taken south all the way to Texas.

☛ The Minnesota Legislature created the nation's first Department of Human Rights.

☞ Minnesota's first form of land transportation for goods was a Red River ox cart.

☞ Johnny Appleseed was said to have come as far west as Minnesota to plant apples.

☞ Eighty percent of the wood harvested in Minnesota becomes paper and paper products.

☞ The pygmy shrew is Minnesota's smallest mammal and weighs the same as a dime.

☞ Al's Breakfast, located in Minnesota's Dinkytown, serves only breakfast and is one of the narrowest restaurants in the state.

☞ According to Minnesota folklore, corn crops should be "knee high by the 4th of July."

☞ The first telegram sent from St. Paul went to the governor of New York.

☞ Temperance leader John Ireland established the first total abstinence society in Minnesota.

☞ It takes 36 seconds for the express elevator to reach the top of the IDS building.

☞ The largest Benedictine monastery in the world is located at St. John's in Collegeville.

☞ Minnesota's average winter temperature is lower than that of Moscow, Russia.

☞ G.A. Hormel Company's workers initiated the first sit-down strike in modern history.

☞ The golden statue of a man atop the capitol building is holding a cornucopia.

☞ Minnesota's Phillips Liquor was the first to emphasize drinking in moderation through a media campaign.

# You Might Be a Minnesotan If...

There are certain unwavering qualities Minnesotans possess. If you are wondering if you are a Minnesotan, here are some warning signs:

☛ The weather is 80 percent of your conversation.

☛ Snow tires came standard on your car.

☛ You measure distance in minutes.

☛ "Down south" to you means Iowa.

☛ You have no concept of public transportation.

☛ Seventy-five percent of your graduating high school class went to the University of Minnesota.

☛ Perkins is the only hangout option in high school.

☛ People from other states love to hear you say words with "o"s in them.

☛ You know what Dinkytown is and where to score drugs once there.

☛ You carry jumper cables in your car—in July.

☛ You drink pop.

☛ The only reason you go to Wisconsin is to get fireworks.

☛ You hear someone say "Ya, sure, you betcha" and don't laugh.

☛ Everyone you know has a cabin.

☛ You assume when you say "the cities," people know where you are referring to.

☛ You have no problem pronouncing the cities Mahtomedi, Wayzata and Edina.

☛ You can list all the Dales (malls).

☛ You know that the numbers 694, 494, 94 and 394 stand for interstates, and you know when to avoid those roads (like all of winter).

☛ You wear shorts when it's 50°F outside in March, but bundle up and complain in August when it gets below 60°F.

☛ You have been trick-or-treating in three feet of snow.

☛ You have gotten frostbitten and sunburned during the same week.

☛ When you say "opener," you're not talking about cans, but the opening days of deer-hunting and fishing season.

☛ You have no problem with the state paying a bounty for killing the state animal—the gopher.

☛ You have licked frozen metal in winter.

☛ You laugh out loud every time you see a news report about a blizzard shutting down the entire East Coast.

☛ You are proud that your state makes the national news 96 nights each year because International Falls is the coldest spot in the nation.

☛ You are excited the first time it snows, and then slap yourself because you know that by April you'll be insanely sick of it.

☛ You have security lights on your front door and garage but leave both unlocked.

☛ Someone in a store offers to help you—and they don't work there.

# I WILL ATTEST TO THAT

*The only thing as varied and dynamic than weather in Minnesota is the people. Who better to say what it means to be Minnesotan than the locals? Here some native Minnesotans share their favorite memories of the state and say what it means to be "Minnesotan."*

## Those Magnificent Minnesotans

*Being from Minnesota, I know two things for sure. I know that 'hot dish' is its own food group, and that no matter what the weather is like, it will never make me change my plans.*

–Jack, Coon Rapids

*Minnesota and our people are easy to both appreciate and make fun of, wholeheartedly. I'm proud to come from a climate of a great pride for the northern work ethic, with such an emphasis on health and education. On the other hand, the Minnesota accent is quite irritating to listen to constantly, and gossip is a common habit for many Minnesotans. Something has to keep people motivated and entertained enough to endure the brutal winters, though.*

–Angie, Stillwater

*What it means to be a Minnesotan is that you are prepared for the change of seasons. The seasons here don't mesh into one or two; we are lucky enough to have four very distinct, drastically different seasons. And sometimes, when you think you're supposed to be wearing your bikini, you're grabbing your coat!*

–Stephanie, Waverly

*Nowhere else can you go boating, ice fishing, camping 'up north,' or justify owning both a motorcycle and snowmobile all while living in the same place!*

–Mark, Cottage Grove

*Minnesota is about being genuine, hearty, self-effacing and proud. It involves loving the sting of freezing nostrils, the frozen echo of vulcanized rubber on wooden boards and being nice to those you don't even know. It's Lake Wobegon, family and old country tradition. Between the Boundary Waters and the Twin Cities there are generations and worlds of difference, but we are all Minnesotans, and that bond means everything in defining us from the rest of the United States.*

–Nathan, Hermantown

*Minnesotans are nice, simply put. There aren't three 'n's in Minnesota for nothing. Also, we're not all riding cows through our farm fields with straw sticking out of our missing teeth; we're a thriving collection of communities that offer the best of all worlds, from the serenity in the deep farm communities to pulsating trendy neighborhoods in the metropolitan areas. Imagine us riding our cows through trendy neighborhoods holding a martini in our BCBG overhauls...that's Minnesota.*

–Jamie, St. Paul Park

*I grew up in St. Paul in what is called the Crocus Hill area. My family believed being from Minnesota meant being 'old shoe,' or in other words, genuine and down to earth. My mother hated any advertising about the benefits of living in Minnesota because she didn't want others to move here. Then there might be 'too damn many people.' When I moved to upstate New York and worked for GE, I was often told how nice I was and then asked if I was like all Minnesotans. Those native New Yorkers could not imagine a state full of nice people, but I can.*

–Becky, St. Paul

# TEN GOOD REASONS TO LIVE IN MINNESOTA

10. It is beautiful. Drive Highway 61 from Red Wing to Duluth during fall, or canoe through the boundary waters in the spring and try not to be moved. I dare you.

9. You won't go thirsty! Having well over 10,000 lakes means there is always something to do on the water. Whether it is water skiing or boating when it's warm, or ice-fishing or pond hockey when it's, well, not—we have the water for it.

8. Minnesotans are ridiculously good looking. Hollywood hotties Jessica Biel and Josh Hartnett can attest to that. And why go to Sweden to see attractive people when you have an entire state filled with Swedish immigrants right here!

7. There's diversity. Whether you like to hike in the woods or attend the latest off-Broadway play, the choices are endless. About the only thing you can't do in Minnesota is be bored.

6. You can shop. Retailers Best Buy and Target got their starts here. And oh, yeah, there is this little place called the Mall of America. (Bonus: No sales tax on clothes!)

5. You can invent. Something in the water makes Minnesotans creative. Rollerblades, buses, Post-It Notes and snowmobiles have all been the result of creative Minnesotans. You could be next!

4.  Sure, the weather is never right; it is either so hot and humid it feels as if you're walking through wet pudding, or so cold your breath freezes as it escapes your body (yes, that can actually happen), but at least it gives you something to talk about. Besides, using your heater and air conditioner on the same day can be invigorating.

3.  Minnesotans are educated! The state has one of the top ranked education systems in the world, and its numerous colleges and universities are ranked in the top 100 in the country.

2.  The people are nice. Go into any store in the state and you are sure to find help quickly. Maybe even from someone who doesn't work there.

1.  You get to learn another language! Words such as "brat," "hot dish" "pop" and a lot of other words with "ice" in them are common, everyday words for Minnesotans. Try using some next time you have the privilege to speak with a Minnesotan. Just don't say "eh"; that's reserved for our crazy friends to the north.

# ABOUT THE ILLUSTRATORS

### Patrick Hénaff

Born in France, Patrick Hénaff is now based in Edmonton. He is mostly self-taught and is a versatile artist who has explored a variety of media under many different influences. He now uses primarily pen and ink to draw and then processes the images on computer.

### Peter Tyler

Peter is a recent graduate of the Vancouver Film School visual art and design and classical animation programs. Although his ultimate passion is for filmmaking, he is also intent on developing his draftsmanship and storytelling, with the aim of using those skills in future filmic misadventures.

### Roly Woods

Roly grew up in Indian River, Ontario. He has worked in Toronto as a freelance illustrator, and was also employed in the graphic design department of a landscape architecture firm specializing in themed retail and entertainment design.

### Graham Johnson

Graham Johnson is an illustrator and graphic designer. When he isn't drawing or designing, he...well...he's always drawing or designing! On the off-chance you catch him not doing one of those things, he's probably cooking, playing tennis or poring over other illustrations.

# ABOUT THE AUTHORS
# & ILLUSTRATOR

### Jeff Neidt

Born and raised in Minnesota, Jeff Neidt is a graduate of St. Olaf College in Northfield, Minnesota. He also studied in Germany and taught creative writing, played hockey and changed his major from German to English while he was there. Jeff enjoys writing, playing hockey and baseball, sampling beers, spending time with his girlfriend and family and watching the local sports teams—even if they do break his heart on a regular basis. Jeff has had his work published in travel and web magazines and is currently a creative writing teacher at a suburban high school.

### Lisa Wojna

Lisa Wojna, author of several other non-fiction books, has worked in the community newspaper industry as a writer and journalist and has traveled all over Canada, from the windy prairies of Manitoba to northern British Columbia, and even to the wilds of Africa. Although writing and photography have been a central part of her life for as long as she can remember, it's the people behind every story that are her motivation and give her the most fulfillment.

### Roger Garcia

Roger Garcia is a self-taught artist with some formal training who specializes in cartooning and illustration. He is an immigrant from El Salvador, and during the last few years, his work has been primarily cartoons and editorial illustrations in pen and ink. Recently he has started painting once more. Focusing on simplifying the human form, he uses a bright minimal palette and as few elements as possible. His work can be seen in newspapers, magazines, promo material and on www.rogergarcia.ca